I0088181

"*Reading with Ralph* is far more than exploring ways to teach reading to an adult. It is the heart warming story of an unlikely relationship—a relationship that developed into a life-changing experience for both teacher and student."

— Jane B. Schulz ED.D, author,
Grown Man Now

"*Reading with Ralph* is a starkly revealing portrait of courage, determination and strength—Ralph's quest to obtain an education is as awe inspiring as Leigh Anne's will to teach him—a reminder to all, that success on and off the football field requires an education, which ultimately serves as a gateway to the world despite one's circumstance in life."

—Coty Sensabaugh,
Defensive Back for the Tennessee Titans
Leukemia & Lymphoma Society

READING
with RALPH

A Journey in

Christian Compassion

LEIGH ANNE W. HOOVER

Reading with Ralph
A Journey in Christian Compassion
Leigh Anne W. Hoover

Published July 2013
Little Creek Books
Imprint of Jan-Carol Publishing, Inc.
All rights reserved
Copyright © Leigh Anne W. Hoover

This book may not be reproduced in whole or part, in any matter whatsoever without written permission, with the exception of brief quotations within book reviews or articles. The inside photographs were contributed.

ISBN: 978-1-939289-20-9
Library of Congress Control Number: 2013943878

You may contact the publisher:
Jan-Carol Publishing, Inc.
PO Box 701
Johnson City, TN 37605
E-mail: publisher@jancarolpublishing.com
www.jancarolpublishing.com

Jan-Carol
Publishing, Inc
"every story needs a book"

For: Brad, Jennifer and Bradley—with special memories of reading together as a family

Reading with Ralph—A Journey in Christian Compassion is dedicated to the many adult and children's literacy tutors who selflessly give of their time and talents to teach reading and serve as frontline warriors against illiteracy. Thank you for your literacy legacy!

Thanks to all of the silent angels who have touched Ralph's life and the many prayer warriors who have encouraged the writing of his story.

Foreword

WHY I ADMIRE RALPH

BY DR. BOB LAUBACH

In 1930 I was a boy of twelve who witnessed a new way of teaching and learning. My parents, Frank and Effa Laubach, were missionaries in the Philippines. My Dad began teaching a group of Muslims on the Island of Mindanao how to read and write in their own language, called Maranao.

At first, Dad employed literate Filipinos to teach the Maranaos. Their salary was only $10.00 or $15.00 a month. But he soon had about 75 "teachers" on the monthly payroll.

The Great Depression of the 1930s caused Dad's Congregational Mission Board to cut his budget in half. No more money to pay teachers! It looked like that promising literacy movement would come to a halt.

Sadly, Dad called a meeting of the Muslim chiefs or *Datus*. One *Datu* proclaimed: "When I learned to read, I did not have to pay anyone. Now, we have no paid teachers. But Dr. Laubach can show me how to be a teacher."

I believe this was a Lord-inspired idea. It worked! A man or woman who learned how to read could sit beside another man or woman and become the teacher.

Dad coined the appropriate phrase for this process: *Each One Teach One*. Now, 85 years later, the motto is not often used. But the system still works!

That is why I admire Ralph and his teacher Leigh Anne! Over the past months they have sat down many times, and the already-literate teacher (I prefer the word "tutor") has led her student, Ralph, on their literacy journey.

Theirs is a journey that is repeated at least ten thousand times each year. We have knowledge of at least 10,000 volunteer "tutors" sitting down beside other "Ralphs" and "Joes" and "Bettys" and "Marias." These tutor-student groups are organized into "literacy councils," of which there are more than one thousand in the USA.

The "mother" council is ProLiteracy, based in Syracuse, New York. ProLiteracy has a national voice to promote literacy among business and government powers. Its New Readers Press develops and publishes a wide variety of teaching materials—the tools that tutors and students require.

Ralph, I will continue to follow your "Literacy Journey." You are inspiring many others to begin the journey into the light of literacy.

– Dr. Bob Laubach
Syracuse, New York

Acknowledgments

Icannot begin to express my most humble appreciation to the many people who have asked about Ralph, sent notes, cards and postcards his way. From the ones who know him to the anonymous who simply extended a gesture of kindness, it has been a pleasure to see this man enjoy receiving mail, reading and learning about others.

It has been truly amazing to watch this little book come together. Thanks are extended to publisher Janie Jessee for her willingness to share Ralph's story in a Christian book. I thank my editor Tammy Robinson Smith for always being on top of every detail and so quickly and graciously addressing each aspect along the way. Tara Sizemore has done an exceptional job with the cover and each photo in the layout.

I am most humbled by Dr. Robert Laubach's foreword to this book and his life's service to literacy and combating illiteracy. Dr. Bob's continued dedication and devotion to spreading the "light of literacy" is simply unparalleled, and I am honored to share his message. This could not have happened without God.

Dr. Robert Laubach is well in his 90s. His father, Dr. Frank Laubach, developed the "Laubach Way to Reading" when he was a missionary. In fact, he was referred to as the "Apostle to the Illiterates." We use Laubach materials at the Literacy Council, and Ralph and I also work with many of the biblical publications.

Thank you to Amy Schmitz and Wallace Barkins at ProLiteracy/New Readers Press for your assistance in connecting me with Dr. Bob. He is such a treasure!

Thank you to *New York Times* bestselling authors Mary Alice Monroe and Patti Callahan Henry for your endorsements and interest in Ralph. You know that I value your friendship and truly admire your work. Mary Alice, you are one special "turtle lady!"

Many thanks are extended to Clemson University and the individuals who helped with the book—Sandra McKinney, Margaret Pridgen, Elizabeth Douglas and Mike Brown.

Thank you to Clemson University's 14th president and Kingsport, Tennessee, native James F. Barker for your endorsement and correspondence with Ralph. My family thanks you and Marcia for your friendship, years of service and for your continued dedication to Clemson.

Thanks to Clemson Head Football Coach Dabo and Kathleen Swinney for the fine, Christian example you uphold for so many and for our "chance" meeting. Your endorsement exemplifies your values and why Clemson University is so blessed. Go Tigers!

Thank you to NFL Titans player and former Clemson University Football player, Coty Sensabaugh, agent and CEO/President Precision Sports Management Group, Christina Phillips and the Sensabaugh family for your efforts and philanthropic endeavors on so many levels.

Dr. Jane Schulz, you are such an inspiration, and I know that Billy sure is proud of his mama. Thank you for your continued encouragement. You are such a jewel.

My senior pastor, Mickey Rainwater of First Broad Street United Methodist Church in Kingsport, Tennessee, has written the afterword, and he very eloquently describes our challenge as Christians.

Finally, to everybody at First Broad Street United Methodist Church, my family members and friends, thank you for engaging me in ongoing conversations about Ralph and for your love. With your support and prayers, this book is finally a reality.

Letter from the Author

Whether it was listening to my third grade teacher, Mrs. Coggins, reading E.B. White's *Charlotte's Web*, or just sharing a special story, I have always enjoyed reading and listening to someone read aloud. Before I was born, my mother was a teacher. When I was a baby, she shared the gift of reading, and I still have some of my books. Mama used to tell me that when I was a little girl, I would say, "Breed [Read] me a book," and she and my Daddy read plenty. In fact, I rubbed all of the fuzz off the "Fuzzy Duckling" Golden Book, but I still have it.

The gift of reading is a priceless treasure and something to be shared throughout our lives. I am thankful that God has blessed me with the gift of writing, and I hope that this little book will be shared and help shine His light for many.

Prologue

Without a doubt, I know that Ralph was placed in my path. Because I answered the gentle nudging and continuing tug of the Holy Spirit, my life has been blessed by communion with a person I would have never envisioned.

It's funny how if we simply open our eyes and ears to the Lord's presence and His work in our lives, we can be enriched in ways never imagined. Ralph has been one such blessing for me.

***

Literacy has always been an interest in my life. As a young girl, growing up in Spartanburg, South Carolina, I co-wrote a neighborhood newspaper with a friend who lived across the street. We decided that neighbors needed to know the news, and this was in the early 1970s, which was long before neighborhood newsletters and social media. Together, we scoured the streets for neighborly news or sales items. At his work, my friend's father would copy the pages that we had typed and Scotch-taped photos. We would assemble and staple the finished product, which was then sold door-to-door for a nickel. The venture filled an early journalistic void for me, and our nominal profits were generously handed over to the South Carolina School for the Deaf and the Blind, where my mother had taught before I was born.

Not until years later, with a degree in secondary education—English—and a minor in general communications, would I have the opportunity to exercise my creative abilities as a journalist and explore my passion for literacy through a nonprofit, volunteer agency, the Literacy Council of Kingsport, Incorporated in Kingsport, Tennessee.

As a board member, I learned all about adult students who, for whatever reason, had failed to learn how to read. Their stories were as individual and compelling as the nightly news, however, each was also alike. Personally, I never planned to actually take a student. In my mind, I was way too busy. However, I did enroll in the offered tutor training to learn more about the organization.

It was hard for me to fathom working with "at risk" individuals and being very much out of my comfort zone. You see, I am considered what is better known as a "germaphobe," and a student would likely make me very uncomfortable. I also have an overbearing fear of head lice, and in my mind, this experience would make me way too vulnerable.

Occasionally, I would notice individuals in our church who benefited from our outreach programs and were invited to come and experience worship. One man sat in front of me and my family for several Sundays, and I noticed him.

CHAPTER ONE

Ralph

Shortly after taking the first portion of the literacy training, I was actually in the Literacy Council of Kingsport office meeting with the executive director when this same gentleman from church walked through the door. Of course, for any prospective student, this first step is the hardest but even more so for him.

Ralph was different and even somewhat frightening. Due to a cleft palate, which had been repaired with a metal plate, and limited hearing, he was always on guard and on the defensive, and he looked mad at the world. At some point, I realized that this man was the person I had noticed at church and the one who we had even previously discussed in a board meeting.

Apparently, he had become outraged at the local library, frightened the staff and was asked to leave. Collectively, we had decided that he was a risk to our nonprofit organization and should not be granted a tutor.

On that particular day, Ralph appeared very distraught and asked if he could speak with us for a moment and tell his story. Although he could barely articulate his need and desire to learn how to read, I knew that I had to help him.

"It's like seeing a kitten in a pet shop window and wanting that animal very badly," explained Ralph. "As much as you wanted that kitten, you knew that you could not have it, and this is how I feel about wanting to read."

With tears in my eyes, I listened to this man's plea, and I felt the overwhelming urge to volunteer to help him. It was no coincidence that I had been noticing him at church, and to beat all odds, he just happened to be bald! No head lice worries; "thank you, God!"

I reached across the table and asked if I could help. Nada Weekley, the executive director, said that she would help him, too.

That was nearly seven years ago and only the beginning of our journey. Ralph and I have met weekly to work on reading and writing and learning about God.

Ralph

CHAPTER TWO

Tutoring

The foundation of the teaching at the Literacy Council of Kingsport, Inc. is the Laubach Way to Reading. Founded by Dr. Frank C. Laubach, an Evangelic Christian missionary often referred to as "the Apostle to the Illiterates," adult volunteers work one-on-one with an adult student, which exemplifies the phrase coined by Laubach, "Each One Teach One."

Knowing that weekly lesson preparations, along with my outside writing and job commitments, would be difficult, I arranged to support Ralph's lesson with additional phonetics, vocabulary, and writing work. I never realized that our weekly sessions would evolve into ministry, but as our friendship grew and trust formed, that is exactly what happened.

In the beginning, just sitting next to Ralph was a little unnerving for me. He was a lot like the main character, Karl Childers, from the 1996 award-winning movie *Sling Blade*, which was written and directed by, and also starred Billy Bob Thornton. Although, I didn't believe Ralph would hurt me, I certainly wasn't taking any chances.

Ralph is my age, and although a lady never tells her age, we are just a few months apart and were both born in 1960. He was the youngest of four boys and born to a middle-class, Catholic couple in Niagara Falls, New York, late in life. According to Ralph, he was deprived of oxygen at birth, due to the umbilical cord being around his neck, and this resulted in brain damage.

All he can remember about early years in school is being taught by nuns and spending much of his time just coloring or sitting in the corner. I know that he was in an environment with nuns because he once shared an old photograph with me, which portrayed a happier time at school on his birthday.

When his mother died, Ralph was only 10-years-old. His father remarried, eventually relocated to Curwensville, Pennsylvania, and for a number of years, he had a stepmother.

Although his graduation year was two years late for his age, and Ralph was only reading very basic words, he did manage to finish high school in Curwensville, Pennsylvania, with a special diploma. He is pictured with the 1980 senior class in the high school annual, and the yearbook is engraved with his name.

Following his father's passing in 1986, Ralph was passed around among siblings, ultimately arriving in East Tennessee to live with an alcoholic, drug addicted brother, who took advantage of his handicap and stole from Ralph's disability income checks.

When Ralph, who was in his late 20s at the time, realized what was happening, he made his escape to the neighboring city of Kingsport, Tennessee, where he found allies in a number of ways and managed to set up a house on his own. From living in a tattered basement apartment, filled with mold from rainwater, to living in a small studio apartment downtown, above a local restaurant, Ralph improvised and began life on his own.

Kingsport is the kind of city where you can safely walk downtown and pop in and out of locally owned and operated businesses. The infamous Church Circle is within walking distance and was planned by design for the Model City by the late American landscape architect

John Nolen. Home to just over 50 thousand, it was the perfect setting for Ralph.

Without a driver's license, he could easily walk or ride his bike to the grocery store, the bank, church and even the Literacy Council. Along the way, he struggled yet managed to have some guardian angel friends cross his path and help with his affairs.

Although, upon initially meeting Ralph, he can appear scary, this is truly a "self-protection" mode, and he has the heart of a child.

Set in his ways, Ralph has strict opinions regarding clothes. He prefers straight jeans, and he has this same style in several colors from the Goodwill Thrift Store, dark tennis shoes, usually a ball cap that he removes indoors, and always a tie—except on Saturdays or when he is home alone. His preferred coat is actually a lined, buttoned work shirt.

Over the years, many have tried to help Ralph with his wardrobe and have generously left clothes and coats for him at the Literacy Council office. Fellow church members worried that he was cold. However, Ralph knows his "style," and all of these items have been promptly taken by Ralph to Goodwill for others. The only item that I know he has kept was a Christmas tie that my husband gave him that depicts the wise men, and he wears it to church during the holidays.

In addition to being bald, which was a great thing for me, Ralph is also a germaphobe, and he obsesses over things. We share this tendency toward obsessive compulsive disorder (OCD), proving God not only answered a prayer. He also "special delivered" us to each other!

When we first began working together, I would carefully unpack my things and occasionally reach for the hand sanitizer. Before long, I realized that Ralph also wanted to use it, and he began cleaning his desk area with it.

At one time, our sessions were scheduled preceding an adult smoker. Even though smoking is prohibited in the Literacy Council office, the smell often lingered in the small classroom. Ralph began spraying the room with Lysol. Of course, he always sprayed much more than was necessary, and when our wait time for the air to clear became increasing longer, we eventually moved our session, and the problem was solved.

The meeting time also changed because I joined a Bible study group, which meets downtown at our church on the same morning. For convenience, Ralph and I moved our meeting time to immediately following Bible study, and we have kept this weekly meeting date ever since.

Ralph with his father

Ralph in middle school

Ralph in high school annual

CHAPTER THREE

Church Directory

Although Ralph was raised Catholic, he has adjusted to being a Methodist, and many on the church staff know him very well. Part of his daily routine is spending hours studying in the church library, and if for some reason the library is not open, Ralph does not hesitate to track down a staff member to open it for him.

Shortly after joining the church, Ralph had his photo added to the church directory. It was a last minute addition before the proof was sent off for publication, so his photo accompanied others unable to sit for a photo and was to be added to the back of the directory.

When the directories arrived for distribution, Ralph was so pleased to be included. His photo discovery moment was similar to Steve Martin's character discovering his name in the phonebook in the movie *The Jerk*. This similar pride lasted until the next directory was published.

Unlike the first appearance, this time Ralph was able to sit for a photo, and he even received the standard, free 8 x 10 copy of his portrait, which he later mailed to an ailing, older brother in Niagara Falls. However, when the new directory was printed, Ralph was angry.

"Ralph, did you see the new directory?" I asked.

"Yeah, I saw it," he grunted.

"Well, did you see your picture?" I asked.

"I'm not in it," Ralph replied. "So, I don't want one."

"What?" I asked. "I'm sure you are in it because you sat for a photo. Remember?"

That Sunday, we borrowed a copy of the directory and looked for his photo. As predicted, his photo was there, but Ralph had only looked in the back and not in the regular alphabetical listings.

Photos had been made during the holidays, so he grinned when he saw his but quickly added, "I should not have been wearing a Christmas tie because it is no longer Christmas."

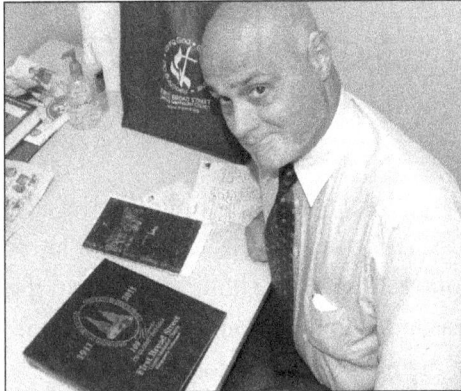

Ralph proudly displays the church directory.

Ralph finds his name and photo in the directory.

CHAPTER FOUR

Sharing our Ministry

T he first Christmas season that Ralph and I worked together, a
member of our worship committee asked if I would share our
story during a special Sunday that was being planned for the traditional
worship service. Four to five members of the congregation were being
asked to share how God had been at work in his or her life.

I have always felt that God put Ralph in my path and referred to
our time together as a type of ministry, but I had never really discussed
it with Ralph.

The next week, I decided to bring up the idea of sharing our story
with Ralph just to get his input and his approval. I also asked Ralph if
I could mention his name and asked if he might stand for others to see
him during worship.

Ralph agreed, and that Sunday as we sat on the pew, he was a nervous
wreck. Each time a listed member would rise and go to the microphone
to share, Ralph would question when my turn would come. My entire
family was anxious for Ralph. Obviously, he had a bulletin, but he was
not able to read my name yet, so this did not help the situation.

Although he struggled extensively with words, Ralph was always pretty good with numbers. So, I told him which number I was in line, and this seemed to pacify him.

When it came time for me to speak, I asked God to help me articulate my message about ministry also being outside of the church walls and sometimes in unexpected places. During my entire time of sharing, I felt the sense of the Holy Spirit and His ultimate guiding of my words.

At the anticipated moment of Ralph's introduction, he suddenly popped up off the pew, and the congregation erupted in applause. Of course, Ralph immediately sat right back down, but as the congregation continued to applaud, he stood back up, clasped his hands together high in the air and began shaking them together while smiling like he had just won a tremendous award.

I am sure Ralph had never experienced an undergirding of support like this. It was definitely a tear-filled moment, and on that particular day, Ralph had, indeed, won the prize.

Ralph in the sanctuary at First Broad Street United Methodist Church in Kingsport, Tennessee

CHAPTER FIVE

Not a Preacher

When Ralph and I first started working together, his favorite activity was using flashcards. In fact, Ralph still enjoys the flashcards today. Like a child, he loves spreading them all out and turning each one over to reveal the word. If he pronounces it correctly, the card goes in a pile on the desk. However, if he misses the word, he immediately turns the card back over to be revealed again later in the game. Ralph always keeps score and knows exactly how many words he has missed.

Another continued favorite has been Bible stories—especially "Jonah." Who has not heard the infamous tale of Jonah and the whale as a child? Ralph had not, and he really enjoyed the story.

Because of Dr. Frank's Laubach's missionary work, many supplementary learning materials at the Literacy Council are Biblical. In fact, a goal for many adult students is to be able to read the Bible.

Following our phonetics work, Ralph and I always incorporate a Biblical lesson. When possible, he will read to me first, and then I will read the very same material from an adolescent Bible. Ralph always closes each of our lessons by reading aloud "The Lord's Prayer."

Ralph is typically moved to tears, and he will always add that, "The reading is very powerful."

On one occasion, I noticed that Ralph seemed troubled by something. During our tutoring session, I asked him if he would like for me to pray with him.

"Ralph, you look like you're concerned about something," I said. "May I pray with you?"

Ralph looked at me and nodded, yet he was quick to add, "But, you know you're not a preacher."

With a big smile, I replied, "Oh, yes, I know that I'm definitely not a preacher, Ralph, but I am sure that God will still listen."

Ralph, Leigh Anne and Brad Hoover teaching Sunday School

CHAPTER SIX

No Presents

After Ralph and I began working together, he would sit with our family during worship. Originally, I would always put either my husband or our son, Bradley, between us. It was still a little unnerving to be right beside him. Yet, when Bradley was away in college, and there were Sundays when my husband served as an usher, invariably, we ended up sitting together. Today, I do not even think about it.

Ralph has also become a member of our Sunday school class. In his mind, it was an opportunity to possibly get to know others and be extended a holiday invitation—especially for dinner. Although there are community events for those without families, Ralph considers himself different, and he does not enjoy fellowship on that level.

As his teacher, I have to keep our relationship on a different level, which means coming to our house is impossible. However, we have taken meals to his apartment and gone out to eat together.

Each year, we sit together at the Christmas Eve candlelight service, and we always take Ralph home because he does not like to walk after dark. Like a child, he loves presents—especially Christmas presents, and he starts making his list early in the year.

The first year I met Ralph, he decided since I am originally from South Carolina, he wanted me to give him some all-cotton socks. These were somewhat difficult to find, but in his mind, a South Carolina girl should have a direct connection to cotton!

Ralph always begins making his rounds in town letting everyone know what he wants for Christmas. Each year, he counts his gifts, saves each one and waits to open them individually on Christmas morning.

The year of the cotton socks, I also decided to get him a rock sculpture of a frog. I knew that he liked them, and I thought he would enjoy the knickknack in his apartment. At that time, I did not realize Ralph is not a hoarder of anything he does not want. He not only takes unwanted clothing to Goodwill, but he also takes unwanted gifts there.

That year on Christmas Eve, he was only in our car for a few moments when he clapped his hands together and declared, "Well, I guess that there are no presents!"

Of course, we had presents for him, including all-cotton socks and a gift shop frog sculpture. Each was neatly wrapped with a matching, handmade bow. When we arrived at his apartment and wished him a "Merry Christmas," Ralph was thrilled to see my adult children pull out wrapped gifts.

It was not until months later that I would learn the frog sculpture from a gift shop had been taken to Goodwill and replaced with a science model of a toad that sat proudly atop his refrigerator in his kitchen.

***

Another year, Ralph decided he wanted to take a present to our church for Jesus. He managed to secure a beautifully wrapped package and specifically asked that it be placed in the church's nativity scene.

In addition to being beautifully wrapped, the special package donned a gift tag to baby Jesus from Ralph, and the whole incident had many anxiously awaiting the opening of Ralph's gift. When Christmas finally arrived, and a person on the church staff had the honor, the beautifully wrapped present was empty.

Concerned, I asked Ralph about his gift, and he replied, "The box was not empty. It was filled with prayers."

Leigh Anne W. Hoover with hugging balloon man, which was a present from Ralph

CHAPTER SEVEN

Very Religious Man

Growing up, Ralph formed very specific views. He has told me that his father taught him to always look over his shoulder, like a hawk, and to be protective of himself.

Ralph believes that men should always wear a tie and remove their hats inside. Although he does dip tobacco, he absolutely detests smoking, drinking alcohol, tattoos, and he vehemently maintains that he is a very religious man. In fact, it has been difficult to compromise with him—especially when it pertains to healthcare.

One year, Ralph was having trouble with his knee swelling, and it appeared that a doctor's visit was imminent. My husband, Brad, agreed to assist Ralph by making an appointment at a church supported, free medical clinic in Kingsport. He also helped Ralph with completing the appropriate paperwork.

On the day of the visit, the attending physician happened to be a friend. He explained further evaluation needed to be done, and tests were necessary to rule out a possible blood clot. In short, this meant the two would be making a trip to the emergency room at the hospital.

Under the very best of circumstances, the emergency room is not somewhere anyone enjoys visiting, and seven hours into it, this was definitely the case for Brad and Ralph. However, the stories from their visit are still being shared today.

After arriving and being admitted to a room, Brad had to convince Ralph that he would have to disrobe and wear a hospital gown. Although this was not an easy task, Ralph trusts my husband, and he complied.

After hours of jockeying with the television remote and turning the channel between "Rocky" and "King Kong" movies, cartoons, and finally, the local news, the technician entered the room.

The next hurdle was convincing Ralph that women are, in fact, very reliable and capable providers, but an ultrasound of his leg took a little more work.

As the technician calmly spoke to Ralph and applied the necessary gel on his leg, the ultrasonic wand proved a little too much for the patient.

Ralph immediately stiffened both legs, retracted to a seated position and very loudly proclaimed, "Stop! You cannot do this. I am a very religious man!"

After being with Ralph for over seven hours, Brad came home after midnight. He was exhausted but happy to report there was no blockage, and Ralph's knee was eventually back to normal.

CHAPTER EIGHT

Postcards

Once Ralph began putting sentences together and increasing his vocabulary, he wanted to read to everyone in town. Periodically, he would make his rounds to share his talents and engage a willing listener. He was so proud.

With this in mind, it occurred to me he might now enjoy receiving mail—especially postcards! Ralph is a member of our Inquirers Sunday school class at First Broad Street United Methodist Church in Kingsport, Tennessee, and he is always a regular attendee. However, due to a cleft palate, which positioned a metal plate in the roof of his mouth, and compromised hearing requiring hearing aids, he has very little interaction with fellow class members.

However, the class is a highly educated, loving and accepting group of Christians, and they are most interested in relating to Ralph on some level. The group also travels quite a bit, and members are often gone both in and out of the country on vacations and business travel.

It occurred to me that "postcards" might be a way to connect with Ralph. Plus, we could incorporate these into our weekly lessons. However, I never realized just how well the activity would work, and it would be as successful as it has been.

Ralph has received postcards from nearly every member of our class, and he has kept each one! Although cursive writing is no longer taught in schools, many in our age range use it often, so the only thing that I request members do is to print.

Postcards have arrived from family beach vacations, ski trips, cruises and trips to numerous foreign countries. In fact, the class has decided it would be fun to display a map on a bulletin board in the class to track Ralph's mail.

With each postcard, Ralph has not only made a reading connection, but he has also personally connected. Through their notes, he has learned about class members and read their names. In turn, I have kept a copy of our church photo directory in my reading bag. Each week, we go through his mail and look for the class members' photos.

Invariably, when we locate a photo, Ralph always exclaims, "I know them! They are in our class at church."

If he happens to miss a word, I can also count on him to say with disgust, "Terrible handwriting," shaking his head. "This handwriting is terrible!"

The funny thing is that the handwriting in question is always impeccable!

Without fail, the postcards of churches are Ralph's favorite ones. In fact, one year, we sent him a beautiful postcard of a breathtaking view from the Grand Canyon. However, Ralph's favorite was one of a cross from Lake Junaluska, North Carolina, that he received at the same time from another member of our Sunday school class.

On a 50th birthday trip to New York, I sent Ralph a couple of postcards. For some reason, the only one that made it to his apartment was the postcard of the little historic church, St. Paul's Chapel of Trinity Church, which survived September 11, 2001. The church served as a respite for firefighters and many others during the tragedy, and today, it is a type of memorial museum.

Coincidentally, the other postcard displaying the lights and fanfare of New York City has still never made it to Ralph's mailbox. Oh well; he would not have cared for this one anyway!

Ralph with all of his postcards in the church library

CHAPTER NINE

Christmas Cards

Christmas is always a difficult time for Ralph. Another of his few cherished possessions is a family photo album depicting past Christmases in a happier time. Even though many embrace Ralph throughout the season, without actual close family members, he feels as if something is missing.

For this reason, I have tried to teach him about the importance of being a member of a church family. We have also talked about how many blessings he has received from those who care about him in the church and in the community and Christmas being celebrated throughout the year and not just on one day.

Knowing Ralph enjoys receiving postcards, one year, I reached out to our congregation at First Broad Street United Methodist Church through our church newsletter. With our senior minister's approval, I wrote a note and asked others if they would consider adding Ralph to their family Christmas card lists. My article explained that we all were truly his only family and that he would appreciate any form of correspondence during the holidays.

Our church family overwhelmingly responded, and Ralph's mailbox was practically overflowing with holiday sentiments from our congregation. In fact, Ralph received nearly 80 cards and letters.

"Leigh Anne, I want you to look at all of my mail!" exclaimed Ralph. "It's unbelievable!"

"Wow! You have a lot of Christmas cards, Ralph," I replied. "Who sent them to you?"

"Most of these are from people at church," said Ralph. "Let me show you."

As Ralph dumped the stack of mail from his book bag, I silently thanked God for this overwhelming outpouring of love. Each card had been carefully opened with a letter opener and returned to its original envelope.

In addition to undergirding Ralph with additional lesson material for our reading sessions, he was filled with the shared love of Christ. With each card, once again, we would cross-reference the names with corresponding photographs in our church directory.

"Ralph, even though you do not have actual blood relatives living near you, all of these people care about you," I explained. "We are all brothers and sisters in Christ, and this is a tremendous blessing."

With tear-filled eyes, Ralph looked at me and said, "Leigh Anne, I am so very thankful. I just don't know what you want me to say."

"You don't have to say anything, Ralph," I replied. "This is just a wonderful blessing! You will have to bring them to Sunday school to share."

Over the next few weeks, we all awaited Ralph's cards. Each week, he would bring in his mail to share with the class, and it was truly a blessing to see the cards connecting Ralph to individuals in a way that previously he never could.

Of course, if the cards were not put back in the exact envelope or passed in the correct order, Ralph would always admonish the offender and quickly get things back on track!

Following the holidays, I submitted a letter of thanks to the congregation explaining how they had really responded, and my article included a photo of Ralph's piled high, holiday mail. The article appeared on the back side of the printed newsletter, which was beside the congregant's mailing address.

To my surprise, Ralph actually noticed the article when his newsletter arrived. He read it, and I heard about it the following week at the Literacy Council!

"Well, Leigh Anne, the congregation really responded with my Christmas cards," said Ralph.

Hearing the very same words that I had written, I immediately looked at Ralph asking, "And, how do you know that, Ralph?"

"How do you think, Leigh Anne?" asked Ralph. "I read it!"

This time, tears filled my eyes because I knew he had, indeed, read at least some of the article.

"I also saw that picture that you took of all my cards," added Ralph.

"Thank you, God," I silently prayed. "Thank you, God!"

Ralph also wrote a special thank you note to the church, and he told me how he feels about his church as follows:

The apartment is not my home. First Broad Street United Methodist Church is my home.

I don't feel lonesome anymore. Jesus is in my heart. All my church people are brothers and sisters in Christ. They send me postcards, birthday cards and Christmas cards. I have saved all of them, and they have helped me with my reading. I am grateful and thank the Lord every day. My life has changed forever.

–Ralph

Ralph's Christmas cards he received in the mail

CHAPTER TEN

Santa's Elf

During Christmas, our Sunday school class always adopts a family. Years ago in high school, Brad had visited a family while wearing a makeshift Santa suit with a beard that just wasn't quite right. He vowed to one day have a suit of his very own.

As a grown man, Brad received a Santa suit from New York as a special gift from his parents and an aunt and uncle. To this day, that special suit is only used for designated Christmas Eve visits. Both of our children have been with him in the role of an elf, and the visits have made an impression on each of them.

When our daughter, Jennifer, accompanied her dad one cold, blustery Christmas Eve, the home was merely cinder blocks, and the windows had garbage bags taped to them to keep out the night air.

In addition to some special toys, clothing and food items are also included so that the family can have a Christmas breakfast and another meal together. The little girl Santa was visiting was so appreciative that she wanted to give something in return.

Jennifer watched as she slipped over into the kitchen and opened empty cabinets. Finally, the little girl located some special cookies, and she brought those, which was all she had, over to share with them.

As a kindergarten teacher, our adult daughter always remembers that special visit that she made with her father, Santa, and the lesson of giving that was shared by one little girl.

Ralph was also able to visit as an elf, and he accompanied Santa as our son, Bradley, drove. They had two families to visit that night, and at each stop, it was hard to distinguish Ralph was, in fact, the elf.

Even though he had the elf hat, Ralph was as excited as the children, and he quickly joined in on the gift giving and the photos. In fact, he wanted to be right in the middle of the family picture with Santa and sit right at his feet!

Ralph and Santa visiting the adopted families

CHAPTER ELEVEN

Toads

Amazingly, Ralph has managed to live alone pretty well. His main complaint is that he does not have a family, and he never ventures out at night. Days are filled with predictable activities, such as dropping by the bank, the newsstand, the Literacy Council, various shops downtown, and, of course, spending lots of time studying in the church library. At night, he watches television, and *Animal Planet* is one of his favorite programs.

Ralph is intrigued by animals—especially reptiles. Like a child, he even pretends that he's part reptile.

"Leigh Anne, you know that I'm not human," said Ralph. "I'm a reptile."

This interest led him to wanting a pet toad. It became his absolute obsession. Ralph would ask every person he encountered if they had seen a toad, and then he would ask again the very next day.

"Have you seen any toads?" asked Ralph. "Oh, OK. I was just wondering."

This became his mantra, and one summer, everyone in downtown Kingsport was looking for a toad for Ralph.

We found the first one, and Ralph was elated. In fact, since he knew you followed the river to get to our neighborhood, in Ralph's mind, we must live in the "fantasy fairyland of frogs!" He was so convinced that he set out on his bicycle to find himself another one.

The next week, Ralph told me he was asked to leave the city park. Apparently, he lost his temper with some people who were also out enjoying a beautiful day.

When I questioned him about his behavior Ralph said, "Well, how did they expect me to ever find a toad when they were all laughing and being so loud?"

Over the years, many have found toads for Ralph. The trick is trying to deliver them to him. Since Ralph doesn't have a phone, you have to hope to find him around downtown or stop by his apartment. At the apartment, you take a chance on Ralph having his hearing aid in to be able to hear his doorbell and come down the flight of steps to the outside. Or, you can throw rocks at his window, like Brad has been known to do, and listen to him say, "You're going to have to pay for the window if you break it!"

Therefore, toads have been left in boxes at the men's clothing store, the bank and the Literacy Council. In fact, one time, a toad escaped from its makeshift home and was loose in the agency overnight! Although the executive director and the volunteer coordinator searched endlessly, they were forced to leave the toad alone until the next morning when it was discovered, by Ralph, crouched in a corner behind a filing cabinet.

Ralph worried and worried about the toad being in the office overnight, but we just told him it also wanted to learn! The runaway toad was red, and that became his name. Ralph later acquired another toad, and he named it Elmo from his other favorite show, *Sesame Street*.

I always wanted to call them frogs, and Ralph would readily correct me stating they were toads and asking if I did not know the difference. Keeping toads as pets required care and compassion, and they also provided a social outlet. Ralph has made numerous trips to the downtown pet shop to purchase crickets. When he has more than one toad, he keeps them in separate aquariums and always monitors their health.

Over the years, he has had about a dozen toads and frogs as pets. Names have included; Elmo, Red, Luck, Leo, Melissa, Kermit, Jonah, Kansas, DC, Tiny Tim, Grover and JoJo. Ralph knows which were released or passed away and the circumstances involved.

In fact, Ralph refers to the toads as his family members. When one becomes ill, or he perceives that it is sick, Ralph has a release ritual, and we are all in mourning for the loss of a family member.

"Leigh Anne, I am very sad today," explained Ralph.

"Oh, I'm sorry. What is wrong?"

"Well, you see, Elmo wasn't doing so good, and I had to let him go today," said Ralph. "I lost a family member."

CHAPTER TWELVE

Death

We had a special man with Down syndrome who was a member of our church congregation at First Broad Street United Methodist Church in Kingsport, Tennessee. His name was Billy Schulz, and everyone knew and loved Billy, including Ralph. When Billy suddenly passed away following surgical complications, his passing greatly affected Ralph. In fact, death has concerned Ralph more than most.

Apparently, in addition to losing his parents, Ralph actually had an elderly person die in his presence, and he has never been the same. Although that person was well into her 90s, Ralph has worried that this will happen to him again.

He works with one of our former Literacy Council trainers, and her age concerns Ralph, too. He was even hesitant to agree to meet for fear that she, too, would die.

So, when his church friend, Billy, passed away at 56-years-old, the death issue arose again. Ralph related to Billy on a level that was different than most. The two had different disabilities, but Ralph truly admired Billy because he knew that, like him, Billy tried and did not let his disability deter his enjoyment of or his involvement in life.

Billy touched lives, and he was an inspiration to many, including Ralph. In addition to holding down a job at the local Food City grocery store as a bag boy, Billy also volunteered as an active usher in our church.

Most importantly, in Ralph's mind, was the fact that Billy always wore a tie. Ralph might wear skintight jeans, which should have been retired years ago, but when out in public, he always wears a tie.

To Ralph, this is a sign of respect, and although he shaves his head and wears a ball cap, he always removes it inside. A tie means so much to Ralph that he does not hesitate to reprimand fellow Sunday school class members when they do not wear one. Billy wore a tie, and he was a hero to Ralph.

We were actually out of town the Sunday Billy's passing was announced, so I knew it would be up to me to tell Ralph. Bible study class members had informed me Ralph was present in worship when the news was announced, but I knew later that day, before our weekly lesson, I would have to also share the news.

As expected, Ralph was sitting on the couch at the Literacy Council waiting for my arrival. When I told him that I had some very sad news, he reacted as many do when receiving such a shock and went into complete denial. In fact, he said that he had heard the news, but he thought that it was Billy's mother who had passed. She had also been ill, and he was certain that was what he had heard.

When I confirmed that it was, in fact, Billy, Ralph visibly shook, shuddered and poured tears of grief for his beloved friend. It was heartbreaking to watch him grieve for someone he viewed as an inspiration. Overtaken with remorse, we decided not to work that day. Rather, we talked about life, death, God's preparing of a place for us and Billy.

His funeral was that weekend, and I told Ralph that I would meet him there. It was an absolutely wonderful service and celebration of such a very special life. The church was crowded, and Ralph actually sat in the pew in front of me during the service. This was a big step for him not to make a scene and have to come sit with me.

Following the service, I had planned to take Ralph home. It was a rainy afternoon, and I did not want him to have to walk. However, Ralph wanted to stay for the reception and to see the video presentation about Billy. Again, this was a huge social advancement for him, so I let him stay.

Ralph is also never one to pass up food. I am sure he was also anticipating piling a plate with goodies, and somehow, I knew Billy must be smiling in heaven.

The next several weeks were also difficult for Ralph. So we worked on writing lessons and talked about eternal life. Ralph was able to articulate what he wanted to write to Billy's mother, and in the lesson sessions following the funeral, we managed to write a sympathy note to her and express his feelings and admiration for her special son.

On several occasions since meeting and working with Ralph, he has expressed the desire to also leave this earthly life, and this has opened the door for me to talk about the timing not being our choice. Rather, we have to trust this is part of God's plan and it's in His hands.

Several weeks passed, and Ralph still talked about Billy and his mother.

"Leigh Anne, let me ask you something," said Ralph. "Do you still have the program from Billy's funeral?"

"Well, actually I think that I might, Ralph," I replied with a tone of question. "Why?"

"You see, I think that I would like to have it if you do. I want to frame it and keep it in my apartment."

When Billy's mother did return to church, she acknowledged Ralph when she came in the sanctuary. I was not there yet, and Brad was serving as an usher. When I arrived to sit beside Ralph, he was visibly shaken.

"Leigh Anne," muttered Ralph. "That older lady spoke to me. Do you see her?" asked Ralph.

As he pointed to the other side of the sanctuary, I noticed Billy's mother, Dr. Jane Schulz. "Yes, Ralph, and you know that she is Billy's mother, right?" I asked.

With that confirmation, Ralph bent over, placing his head on the pew in front of him and wept. It was the release of raw emotion from a grown man with the caring heart of a child.

Immediately, I excused myself and went over to share his sentiments. The next week, I received a note from her in the mail with a sentence written especially for Ralph. He also received a personal note from Jane, which we read together in our lesson, and the two have continued greeting each other weekly at church.

Ralph eventually located a copy of the program with a color photo of his beloved friend from the funeral, and he brought it to his lesson in a special frame.

Prior to Billy's passing, he and his mother were notified that they would be receiving honorary doctorates from Western Carolina University in Cullowhee, North Carolina, for their tremendous work in the field of Down syndrome and special needs persons. Jane accepted this award and received Billy's honorary doctor of humane letters posthumously for her dear son. You can read about their life in Schulz's book *Grown Man Now*.

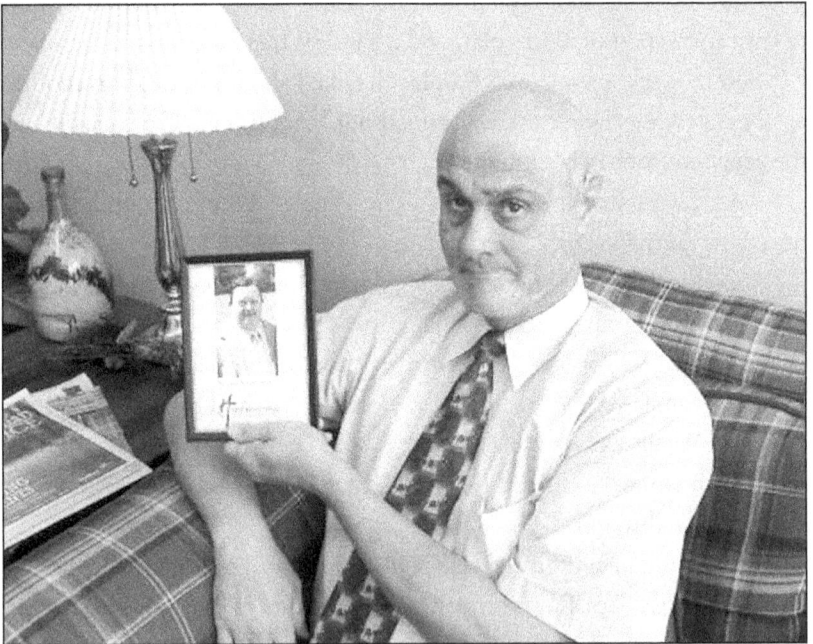

Ralph holding the framed program from Billy Schulz's funeral

CHAPTER THIRTEEN

Heaven

If anyone has the right to complain about life, it would certainly be
Ralph. He is hesitant to share his background and always attests that
it brings up bad memories. As the fourth son born to an aging couple later
in life, he already faced looming obstacles. Yet, with a cleft palate, limited
hearing, and a host of learning disabilities, his life journey would prove
challenging in the best of circumstances.

In fact, one of the last comments he remembers before setting out on a
solitary life was a brother's threat that he would never make it living alone
because he is "retarded." Despite unfavorable circumstances, Ralph has
prevailed. He is even somewhat domesticated and cooks his own meals.

Without a dishwasher, Ralph prefers purchasing disposable pans
instead of washing. Many of our weekly lessons begin with questions about
what he's been cooking. For some time, Ralph believed that he needed to
avoid pork for religious reasons. However, when I assured him that both
Methodists and Catholics do eat pork, he seemed appeased and has since
added ham to his cooking repertoire.

Ralph's early childhood was spent in Catholic schools with nuns. I
know this is true because he has shared photographs of himself with

the nuns celebrating his birthday in a classroom setting. I have often asked how he was able to be in school yet not learn how to read. Frustrated, Ralph will say that I ask too many questions and explain that he spent a lot of time drawing with crayons.

Actually, Ralph is a pretty good artist, and I have been able to talk him into drawing a few things for me. Once he drew a buffalo head for me on the church bulletin to tell me that he had purchased bison meat at the grocery store. He is also good with numbers and seems to have adapted better to simple math in school verses reading and writing.

When he feels frustrated, Ralph will occasionally talk about being ready to go "home" to heaven. I will ask him to talk about his concerns with his life and ask God to give me the necessary words to encourage this man.

I have also realized many in his place might feel very discouraged with living. With this concern, I have simply tried to tell Ralph God knows our earthly lives can be difficult, and He is preparing us for a life with Him one day. Only God knows when this will be, and it is not our decision.

"Leigh Anne, I know, but it is so hard," explained Ralph. "I don't like living in the city. I need to be in the country, and what am I going to do when I am old?"

"Ralph, I understand," I answered. "But, let's think about all of the great things that you do have. Do you remember your list?"

Several years ago, Brad and I decided we all three needed to go to lunch together after church and really talk about Ralph's life. He seemed deeply troubled, and quite frankly, his ongoing anxiety had me and others very worried.

Together, we made a list of all of the good things in Ralph's life. Of course, in addition to his apartment, his bicycle and his friends at church and around town, his toad was also listed.

Ralph does not have a driver's license or a vehicle, so he frequently walks to where he needs to go in town or rides his bike. Occasionally, he will also ride the public transportation. However, because he is always on the defensive, Ralph is often fearful of this, too.

Once his list was made, Ralph agreed he does, in fact, have many blessings, and his life is not that bad. He also knows our reward of heaven is

God's promise. God has prepared a place for us, and He will decide when it is time for us to be with Him.

"Ralph, we are told not to worry about tomorrow," I explained. "None of us knows what our future holds, but God does, and we have to trust Him. This is faith, Ralph, and God is always with us through the Holy Spirit. Do you understand?"

"OK, Leigh Anne," answered Ralph. "But, what will happen to me when I die?"

"That is something that we need to talk about," I explained. "And you can help with these decisions."

"All right," he replied. And, you know I love you, right?"

In the following weeks, Ralph discussed death plans at church and even with the local funeral home. Once he found out Billy Schulz had been cremated and had a permanent resting place in the columbarium at our church, this became Ralph's plan, too.

Rather than wondering how the state might provide for his funeral, Ralph actually walked to the funeral home, which is next door to the church, and obtained cost details that he brought to his lesson to share with me.

"Leigh Anne, I need to show you something," said Ralph.

"Sure," I replied. "What do you have there, Ralph?"

As he pulled out a small sheet of paper with printed numbers, I realized that it was an outline of anticipated funeral expenses.

"Well, you see," began Ralph, "Since Billy passed away, I have been wondering about my funeral, and I have some information."

"Where did you get this, Ralph?" I asked.

"I got it at the funeral home, Leigh Anne. This is what I want, and I want to be beside Billy at the church," Ralph replied.

"Oh, is Billy in the columbarium?" I asked.

"He is, and I will show you," said Ralph.

That Sunday, as the rain sprinkled down on the courtyard, Ralph motioned for me to come over to the door leading outside.

When he caught my eye, I knew he was motioning me outside to show me Billy's place in the church columbarium.

"Right here, Leigh Anne," said Ralph. "Do you see Billy's name? I want to be beside William Robert Schulz."

Realizing that there were several positions beside Billy, I told Ralph I felt like we could make sure this would happen and prayed another silent prayer of thanks to God.

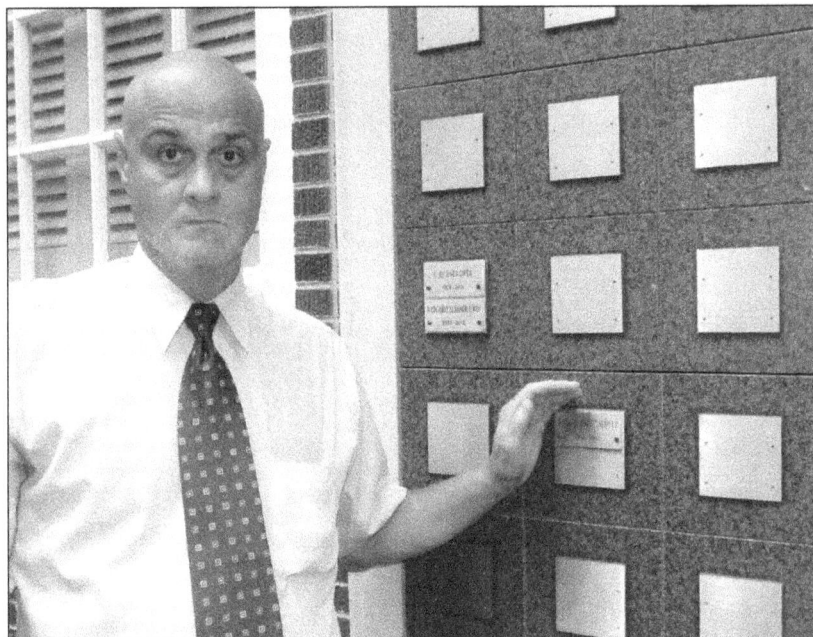

Ralph stands beside Billy Schulz's resting place at First Broad Street United Methodist Church in the columbarium.

CHAPTER FOURTEEN

State Disability Requirements

My husband is a banker downtown, and Ralph is a frequent visitor and customer. He actually banks with two local banks and does well with money. In fact, he is often penalized by our government for managing his disability check and saving money.

Unfortunately, because he has done the right thing by saving, Ralph does not qualify for a free telephone or even for food stamps. Rather, he goes without one and buys groceries based on what he receives.

If I get a phone call from the local newsstand, chances are it's Ralph trying to contact me. However, he never leaves a message and will call until he gets me or move on and call another friend.

One day, he came into the bank very upset and asked to see Brad. He had received notification from the State of Tennessee that his disability had not been reviewed in over 20 years, and he was at risk of losing his benefits.

Ralph was able to read just enough to become fearful and emotional saying if this were to happen, he could not even live.

"Brad, I have to have my check. What does this mean?" asked Ralph.

"I don't know, buddy, but don't worry," explained Brad. "We will figure this out together, and I will help you."

Brad immediately called the state office to plea Ralph's case and explained his connection to Ralph was through his wife being his tutor at the Literacy Council.

"That should tell you something right there," explained Brad. "He cannot even read what has been sent to him, but he can make out enough to know that he has reason to be concerned."

Brad was able to arrange for a conference call, and the representative heard Ralph speak and inquire about the papers.

The state official proceeded to explain his records had not been reviewed, for whatever reason, in over 20 years. Although he was unable to read, the paperwork would still need to be completed and returned for review.

As requested, we did this, and Brad followed up with the state to make sure that Ralph continued to receive his benefit check. In order for this to happen, Ralph had to completely trust Brad. It was amazing to witness God at work to assist this man.

Ralph with Brad Hoover

CHAPTER FIFTEEN

Lunch Date

W hen Brad and Ralph began to form a friendship, Ralph was somewhat hesitant. He was not used to two men being seen together, especially at lunch, and he worried others might think they were on a date.

"Leigh Anne, why can't you go eat with us?" asked Ralph. "I am a very religious man, and I do not go out with a man."

Laughing, I replied, "Ralph, it's not a date. Businessmen go out to lunch together all of the time."

"Well, I will just feel better if you would go, too," said Ralph.

So, the three of us decided to go to a Chinese buffet for lunch. In the restaurant, Ralph was thrilled. He could go through the line as many times as he liked and eat all sorts of things.

It's really rather sad to see him eat because it is like he will never have another meal. Like a child, I remind him to put his napkin in his lap and to eat slowly. Yet, like a child, he rarely remembers.

"Slow down, Ralph." I said. "You have plenty of time to eat, and please use your napkin."

"OK, sorry," he replied. "Hey, do you think one of those Chinese women might walk on my back? No, um, I'm just teasing, but my back hurts."

As we were eating, a young Asian man came over to our table to ask if we were doing all right. When talking with us, he explained he was the manager because he was one of the only employees fluent in English.

Noticing that his English was really good, and several Hispanic customers were also in the restaurant, I asked if he also spoke Spanish.

Immediately, Ralph thought I had insulted the manager, and he lunged across the table putting his arm out towards me.

"Excuse her!" he exclaimed. "She does not understand."

In the midst of all of this commotion, I was laughing so hard tears were literally streaming down my face.

"Leigh Anne, you are so rude," stated Ralph. "Look at his eyes," Ralph explained and pulled at his own eyes to demonstrate the Asian eye. "Can't you see that he is not Mexican? And, why are you laughing and crying? You are embarrassing me, and you're not coming back!"

Later that day, Ralph reported my behavior to the Literacy Council. To this day, he still does not understand why I asked the man about speaking Spanish, and occasionally, Ralph will remind and reprimand me for this.

CHAPTER SIXTEEN

Food City

I have always admired the Food City Grocery family. They are a wonderful, family-owned operation, and over the years, Food City has given thousands of dollars back to the region. The organization upholds the highest standards in operations, and they have been a tremendous supporter of literacy.

When my first children's book, *The Santa Train Tradition*, was published, Food City a partner of the Santa Train program of the Kingsport Area Chamber of Commerce, agreed to sell the hardback book in their stores along the 110 mile route from Shelby, Kentucky, to Kingsport, Tennessee. My hope was that a portion of the proceeds would benefit the Santa Train Scholarship, which is awarded annually to a graduating high school senior along the route, and the Literacy Council of Kingsport. I never imagined the grocery store would donate 100 percent of their proceeds, and to date, the sale of that little book has generated over $10,000 for the Santa Train Scholarship.

So when a new Food City store was locating in downtown Kingsport, I was thrilled. However, no one was happier than Ralph.

"Hey, Leigh Anne," called Ralph. "You know something? Food City is opening downtown!"

"I know, Ralph. Isn't that exciting?" I replied.

"Yep, just a few more weeks, and I can't wait!"

He literally was counting the days until the new store opened. For Ralph, this meant another easily accessible place that could be added to his weekly route around town.

Often, Ralph would take a taxi cab to the grocery store, which was another Food City location in town, and the driver would wait while he shopped. Ralph would buy lots of items at once, and he would freeze purchases so he did not have to shop as often.

For this reason, he was leery of taking public transportation because he would have so many bags.

One day, he went to Food City on his own and called a cab to pick him up. Yet when the driver arrived, Ralph sent him on his way.

"Leigh Anne, this cab driver showed up to get me, and he had tattoos all over his arms," explained Ralph. "He opened his trunk, and it was filthy. I told him to, 'just go on.' Sorry, but I was not riding!"

Ralph does not like tattoos at all. Although most would think he might be the type to have one, if there is even a type, but he is very conservative and does not believe in these at all.

Faced with a dilemma and lots of purchased groceries, Ralph pulled out his handwritten call list of a few friends, used the store's phone and located someone who was willing to pick him up and take him home.

I really had to talk to Ralph about this because I explained he was inconveniencing others by calling like this. He had a hard time understanding the problem, but seems to be doing better.

Again, because he is very set in his ways and is a man of routine, he still prefers to buy groceries in this manner yet does seem to make more frequent trips since there is now a store located downtown.

"I'm a happy man!" said Ralph. "Yep, Food City has opened, and it is great! "I'm a happy, happy man."

Shortly after the opening, however, his excitement quickly waned. Apparently, someone matching Ralph's description was asking patrons for money in the grocery store parking lot downtown. This was reported to the store manager, and they mistakenly thought the guilty person was Ralph.

The offender may have matched Ralph's physical description, but the man certainly did not have Ralph's heart.

"Brad, I need to talk to you," Ralph said as he entered Brad's office at the bank. "I know that you're a very busy man, and I don't want to hold you up, but I need you," he said with tears filling his eyes.

Brad quickly ushered Ralph into his office saying, "Of course, Ralph, what's wrong, and how can I help you?" asked Brad.

"Well, you see," began Ralph, "I was in Food City, and the manager thought that I had been asking people for money in their parking lot."

"Why would he think that, Ralph?" asked Brad concerned.

"I don't know, but Brad I NEVER did that," said Ralph.

"OK, I believe you," answered Brad. "I know the store manager, and he's a great guy. Let's go pay him a visit."

Together, the two loaded up in Brad's vehicle and drove over to the store. As always, the manager was in and more than happy to meet. Instead of staying in the store aisle, Brad asked if there was somewhere private the three could talk, and the manager escorted them to a more private meeting room.

Once seated, Ralph immediately began to cry again as Brad explained what had happened. Fortunately, Brad knew Ralph's heart, morals and mannerisms, and he knew he could speak to Ralph's character.

Food City always puts customer service first and foremost in everything. The business goes above and beyond to make each and every customer feel welcome and comfortable shopping in their stores. Store managers know most of their customers on a first name basis, and customer satisfaction is guaranteed.

Employees share an unrivaled camaraderie. In fact, some of the Food City stores' employees are even adults with special needs. Ralph's friend, Billy Schulz, worked for Food City a number of years during his lifetime as a bagboy. So, Brad knew that this situation was certainly a rarity for the store, and they would want Ralph to feel welcome as a customer.

After pleading his case, the manager also noticed Ralph's emotional response and immediately knew that the offender could not have been Ralph. He felt certain this was another person.

When the meeting concluded, the manager extended a sincere apology to Ralph and said he was welcome to shop in Food City anytime. Ralph's smile returned, and he left a "happy man." To this day, Food City is still Ralph's favorite grocery store, and it's mine, too.

Santa Train Scholarship first check presentation - 2009
Left to Right: Food City Store Manager Ed Moore, author Leigh Anne W. Hoover and (retired) Food City Senior Vice President of Marketing Tom Hembree
In memory of Ed Moore

CHAPTER SEVENTEEN

Golf

Ralph and Brad share a special friendship, and Ralph knows he can trust Brad. There is a mutual admiration between them. Brad admires Ralph's determination and his work ethic, and Ralph shares the same respect for his friend.

Although Ralph has never played golf, he knows it is a game and hobby Brad enjoys. For this reason, he requested a book about golf to read aloud with another tutor, and he was so proud to learn about the game.

In fact, Ralph began spotting and collecting random golf balls he would find around town and saved them for Brad. It was not uncommon for Ralph to bring a few to Sunday school in a grocery bag for his friend, and the two would talk about golf.

One year, Brad decided to surprise Ralph and take him to play putt putt for his birthday. It would be a guys' outing and they would go eat and then introduce Ralph to golf through the game of putt putt.

As mentioned, Ralph is very methodical with everything he does, and of course, he approached putt putt in the same manner. On the

Ralph playing putt putt

other hand, Brad likes to tease Ralph when he can, and this presented the perfect opportunity.

While the two made their way around the putt putt course, and Brad explained the game to Ralph, he would wait for Ralph to take his turn, and then, Brad would address the ball. However, Brad hit the ball horribly and on purpose.

"Brad, what are you doing?" Ralph asked as Brad's golf ball ricocheted off the wooden sides of the marked pathway of the course. "You're worse than I am!"

Brad remained calm and said, "What do you mean, Ralph?"

"Well, just look at your shot," Ralph replied. "You're horrible!"

"Is that right?" asked Brad. "Why don't we play another round then? Are you in?"

"Brad, I think so, but my stomach's really hurting," he replied.

Like other lunch and dinner outings, Ralph had really enjoyed himself, especially this night because it was his birthday celebration.

The two agreed they would play another round, but they would have to pick up their pace. As they made their way around the course once more, Ralph became increasing agitated.

"Ralph, are you OK?" Brad asked.

"Maybe not, Brad," he answered. "Um, my stomach hurts."

"Why don't we call it a night then, buddy?" Brad asked. "Let's go."

As the pair made their way back and loaded up in Brad's 4-wheel drive vehicle, Ralph squirmed and grimaced with every bump taken in the road.

"Take it easy, Brad," said Ralph. "Oh, my stomach hurts."

Knowing Ralph would likely refuse because of his fear of germs, Brad still asked, "Do you need for me to pull over and stop somewhere?" "I can if we need to, Ralph."

"No, just keep going," he said. "Um, but watch those bumps," replied Ralph holding his stomach.

When the vehicle finally pulled in front of Ralph's apartment, he flew out as quickly as Brad came to a stop.

"Gotta go, Brad," said Ralph. "Thanks! See ya!"

***

The next day, Ralph arrived for his lesson at the Literacy Council, and he was as white as a sheet. Apparently, it had been a difficult night for him, and he was totally swearing off Chinese food.

"Leigh Anne, I am never eating Chinese food again," said Ralph.

"Really, you don't look well," I replied. "What happened?"

"Brad took me to eat, and the food was bad," Ralph replied.

"Are you sure this didn't have something to do with the amount of food you ate?" I asked.

"No, that food was bad," said Ralph. "It had me up all night, and I'm never going back."

***

To this day, he still refuses to eat Chinese. However, golf remains an interest. For Brad's birthday, Ralph was so proud. Instead of bringing golf balls he had found, he happened upon some in a store, where the balls were sold in an egg carton.

"Got Brad some golf balls for his birthday, Leigh Anne," Ralph said proudly as he smiled, nodded and shook his head.

"You did?" I asked. "Well, that was very nice of you, Ralph."

"Sure did," he replied, still smiling. "I left them on his desk at the bank in an egg carton."

The balls were practice round, range golf balls, but Ralph didn't know, and Brad didn't care. It truly is the thought that counts, and this was one of his best birthday presents ever!

Ralph and Brad on Brad's 50th birthday

CHAPTER EIGHTEEN

Birthdays

L ike a child, Ralph looks forward to almost each and every holiday. However, he does not particularly care for Valentine's Day.

He especially enjoys his birthday. When I first met him, Ralph started telling me the date of his birthday early on, and I made note of it on my calendar. As the date approached, the mentions became more frequent.

I decided that it would be fun to invite others from around town to drop by the Literacy Council office for cake and to wish Ralph a happy birthday, but we would keep the party a surprise for him.

Others were more than willing to help make his day special and offered to assist with the decorations and the goodies. Because he likes toads, we arranged for his cake to have two toads made of icing. One was larger and red for the toad named "Red," and the other was a smaller, green one, which was "Luck."

Ralph was told to come by the office to get a present, and he walked in to a room with about 10 to 12 friends. Immediately, his eyes filled with tears of joy and appreciation.

"Is this all for me?" asked Ralph. "All of you are here for my birthday?"

"Yes, Ralph," I answered. "You are the guest of honor, and everyone is here to wish you a happy birthday!"

With that, we all began to sing. Ralph cried, and with fingers in the air, he conducted our singing while singing along.

"Look... is this my birthday cake?" he asked.

"Yes, it is," I replied. "Come look at what's on it, Ralph."

As he peered over the large sheet cake, he exclaimed, "It's a toad!"

"No, two toads," said Ralph. "That red one is my toad, Red, and the smaller one is Luck."

According to Ralph, toads and frogs are very different, and he always manages to remind me of this. Everyone knows that toads are not in the water like frogs! Although the cake decorator had placed them on lily pads like frogs, surprisingly, Ralph refrained from pointing out this error on his birthday, and he posed for photos proudly beside his special birthday cake.

Ralph with his frog birthday cake

CHAPTER NINETEEN

Bays Mountain

As a journalist, I have the pleasure of writing a monthly column in *East Tennessee Medical News* titled "Enjoying East Tennessee." During the fall, I planned to feature Tennessee's largest city-owned park and the newly renovated state-of-the-art planetarium at Bays Mountain Park and Planetarium in Kingsport.

I thought that it would be exciting for Ralph to come along with me, so I gained permission from the director. Prior to our going, I told Ralph a little about Bays Mountain, and he seemed excited to go.

Of course, like a child, I cannot tell him about such outings too far in advance, or he asks about it every day until we go. So, about a week before, I confirmed the appointment, checked the extended weather forecast and planned our outing.

Leading up to the trip, which happens to be just about 15 minutes outside of downtown Kingsport, Ralph became concerned he might need more details. He stopped in the Literacy Council office to ask Nada, the executive director, if she knew anything about Bays Mountain and if he needed to pack a bag.

He was also increasingly anxious my husband, Brad, would not be able to join us. Ralph dropped in the bank to personally invite Brad to go with us.

On the day that I picked him up outside of his apartment, Ralph got in my car and asked about Brad.

"Hello, Leigh Anne," said Ralph. "I really appreciate you taking me to Bays Mountain."

"You are welcome, Ralph," I answered. "I'm just glad that you are going with me."

"Why is Brad not going?" he asked.

"Well, Brad has to work today, Ralph," I replied. "This is my job, and I am glad that you can go on our field trip."

Ralph accepted my answer, but I could tell that he was still a little disturbed.

"How long do you think it will take to get there?" he asked.

"Oh, not too long," I answered. "Remember, it's just a short drive up the mountain."

"Really?" asked Ralph. "I didn't ever know that."

As we continued our drive and began to make our way up the mountain to the park entrance, Ralph looked out the window and noticed everything.

"Leigh Anne, I never knew that this Bays Mountain was even up here," said Ralph.

Once we checked in with the park entrance, I was told to go on up to check-in at the Nature Center. After parking the car and securing what we would need for the afternoon, we were on our way. However, Ralph suddenly stopped.

"Leigh Anne, I need to tell you something," said Ralph.

"Sure; what is it, Ralph?" I asked.

"Leigh Anne, you do know that this is not a date," said Ralph.

"Ralph, I know, and what did I tell you that this is?" I asked.

"A field trip," he mumbled. "Right? 'Cause, I mean you're a married lady, and I'm a very religious man!"

As always, I tried not to let him see me laugh, and I reassured him that I certainly knew and decided that was why he kept insisting that Brad should go.

Once this was understood, the childlike wonder returned. When Ralph came upon the first park signage, he read it aloud to me with delight.

"Leigh Anne, I can't believe I read that," said Ralph as he studied the wooden sign.

"I know, Ralph," I replied. "I am so proud of you, and this is why all of your hard work has been so important."

Right there, in front of that signage, I thanked God for the opportunity to have this man in my life and for the chance to share the gift of reading.

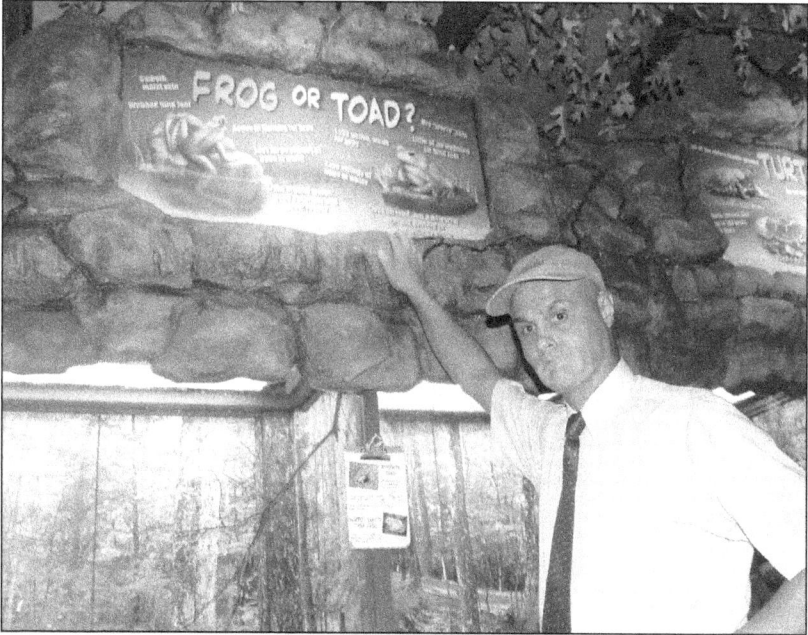

Ralph in the Herpetarium at Bays Mountain

CHAPTER TWENTY

Apartment

For as long as I have known Ralph, he has lived in a tiny, upstairs studio apartment downtown. It's very small, but from what he has told me, this is the best living accommodation he has experienced since being out on his own. Others downtown within his price range were riddled with problems, so being small does not seem to bother him.

The first time that I saw it, I was surprised at his neatness. Although he prefers to sleep on a mattress, which is on his floor, versus having a bed, he is quite content, and the makeshift bed is always made and very neat.

Last year, on Christmas Eve, Brad and I were invited up to his apartment with our two adult children, Jennifer and Bradley. Ralph wanted us to see his large Christmas bear, which was purchased at Food City. Although we always take him home after the Christmas Eve candlelight service at our church, we rarely go inside, and our children had never been inside of Ralph's apartment.

That night, he spoke about his bear again, and we asked if he would like for us to see it. Ralph was so proud to take our family in his apartment.

"Take your shoes off before coming inside," requested Ralph as he pulled off his black tennis shoes and placed them in a pasteboard box just inside his door.

With perplexed looks on their faces, my children wondered if they should comply.

I said to Ralph, "We will only be in for a minute. Would it be OK, just this one time, to leave them on?"

Reluctantly, Ralph agreed and mumbled for us to come on inside.

Even though there is only a small kitchen, living room and tiny bathroom, everything was in order and set in its place. From the small table to the neatly made bed on the floor, it was in order.

The first time that I visited, I noticed a similar semblance of order, yet a wooden bread box was nearly white with dust. Shelves were also coated with a layer of dust, but the stove and countertops were spotless.

Ralph mentioned that dust was natural. However, since he suffers from apparent nasal allergies, I suggested that he might try Pledge wipes. I even gave him a package and showed him the word "allergens" on the back and asked him to read it. From that moment on, I believe dusting became part of his cleaning routine, and that night, I was pleased to see the bread box appeared to have been dusted.

As we entered the small apartment, Ralph beamed with pride. We had never seen his tabletop Christmas tree or the little Christmas village figurines. Again, every item was meticulously in its place, and the large, white stuffed bear was proudly sitting in his only chair.

"There he is!" declared Ralph, as if we might just miss him. "His name is Poland because he is a polar bear."

"Wow! He's really big," said our daughter, Jennifer. "He looks great in your chair."

"Thank you, Jennifer. Do you see my presents?" asked Ralph, as he added our wrapped gift.

Like a child, Ralph greatly anticipates Christmas, and he really enjoys presents. He keeps them under his tree and waits to open each one on Christmas morning.

After the first Christmas, we told him that he really should not ask for gifts, but if people ask him what he would like, he may give suggestions. However, he should not give the same idea to every person.

I knew the children felt touched to be included in Ralph's world, and they were deeply moved by the experience. In addition to his personal items, he also mentioned his mail and talked about various cards and postcards. Several postcards from the past year were displayed on his refrigerator with magnets, and our son, Bradley, was moved to see one he had sent to Ralph during a study abroad at Oxford with Clemson University among them.

Ralph with Poland bear during Christmas

CHAPTER TWENTY-ONE

Clemson

My husband and I met and began dating while students at Clemson University. We actually met in student senate and since our collegiate years have remained involved with the university.

While our children were in college at Clemson, we were members of the Parents' Development Board. In fact, our involvement with the organization began with a "God instance" on the beach.

We were on Hilton Head Island, South Carolina, as a family for a conference I was attending. When the meeting was over, we extended our trip for beach time. During the afternoon, our younger child, Bradley, who was in middle school aspiring to one day attend Clemson, was playing on the beach in his Clemson tiger paw bathing suit when he met Clemson University Associate Dean of Students Rusty Guill.

Little did we know, but Rusty Guill connects students, families and others to Clemson on a regular basis, and he always shows up, whether it's around campus activities or on move in day, when needed. We affectionately refer to him as a "Touched by an Angel" kind of guy from the once popular television program.

When Rusty noticed Bradley's "tiger paw" bathing suit, a conversation ensued, and he immediately asked him about Clemson. At the time, his sister, Jennifer, had just completed her freshman year at the university.

As we walked up to the two chatting on the beach, we also discussed Clemson and remained in touch with Rusty, who got us involved with Clemson University Student Affairs and the Parents' Development Board.

Being ambassadors for our alma mater has been a true delight, and our blood really does run a darker shade of orange. In fact, the 14th president of Clemson, James F. Barker, and his wife, Marcia, are actually Kingsport natives, which is another wonderful connection. However, despite the ongoing rumor, being from Kingsport does not guarantee admittance or in-state tuition. Yet, if someone is privileged enough to be a "Tiger," it certainly does instill pride and the essence of family.

In the true Clemson spirit, Ralph has become a fan on many levels. Although he has never visited the campus, he knows all about Clemson, and during football season, he proudly wears his orange t-shirt—especially on "solid orange" Fridays and sometimes again on Sunday under his dress shirt.

If you look closely, it's not hard to spot the CLEMSON lettering across his chest under the Friday dress shirt. Ralph knows to wear the orange Clemson t-shirt that we gave him on Fridays, but since he always wears a dress shirt and a tie in public, this presents a bit of a problem. Therefore, he wears his Clemson t-shirt as his undershirt and will occasionally give others a glimpse of his t-shirt if asked.

One day, as Ralph sat outside of a corner cafe, a visiting patron asked about his orange.

"I see you are wearing orange," stated the customer. "You must like UT [University of Tennessee]."

"No," mumbled Ralph followed by an angry expression. "Not UT. I'm a Clemson man, myself."

Ralph is not a sports fan, but when professional football player and Kingsport native, Coty Sensabaugh, was playing football for the Tigers, Ralph became even more interested in Clemson.

When the *Kingsport Times-News* did an article on Sensabaugh, Ralph was able to read some of the feature, and the young athlete's words of determination quoted in the article literally brought Ralph to tears.

"Leigh Anne, I can't believe it," said Ralph. "He [Sensabaugh] says the same thing about playing football that I say about learning to read."

"I know, Ralph." I replied. "I thought that you would appreciate this article."

"He says that it takes dedication, determination and continued practice to succeed on the field," continued Ralph. "I can't believe it! That's what I say and what I have to do every day to learn how to read. It just takes patience. Patience..."

From that moment forward, the smile across Ralph's face assured me that he would maintain his own determined spirit just knowing that others fought hard for their goals, too.

Filled with complete pride, Ralph posed for a photo with the newspaper on his desk, and that picture made its way to numerous inboxes via email, including that of Clemson University President James F. Barker.

As Clemson family members always do, notes of mutual pride were exchanged, shared and expressed about Ralph. However, one very special note arrived in Ralph's mailbox, and this one was from President Barker.

Although Ralph originally thought that the note, penned on "President's home stationary," was from the President of the United States, he was just as elated to learn that it was from the president of Clemson University and that President Barker was, indeed, also proud of him.

In fact, we had to make copies of the note at the Literacy Council so that Ralph could take it to church and all around town in Kingsport to share with others.

"Leigh Anne, this note says that President Barker is from Kingsport," said Ralph.

"I know, Ralph. Can you believe it?" I asked.

"I didn't know that," Ralph replied. "And, he saw my picture!"

Ralph showing his Clemson shirt

Ralph reading the article in the newspaper about Coty Sensabaugh

CHAPTER TWENTY-TWO

Barker Card and Letter from Ralph

Shortly after the winter semester of 2013 began at Clemson University, President Barker discovered that he was going to have to undergo heart bypass surgery. Barker is an athletic man and can often be spotted on campus running with his Labrador, "Mookie." He's also done pushups in the Tiger mascot suit at football games. So, students were surprised to learn about the impending surgery and to later hear that he actually underwent five heart bypass procedures.

The following week when Ralph and I met for our lesson, I updated him on President Barker's situation, and I told Ralph that he was taking a leave of absence from Clemson during his convalescence.

Ralph was also very concerned, so I asked if he would like to send President Barker a card and write him a letter.

"Ralph, if we have a get well card in the office, would you like to write a note to President Barker?" I asked.

"Oh, sure, sure, Leigh Anne," said Ralph. "Yes, I would like to do that."

After securing a card and making sure that it had just the right sentiment, Ralph began to verbally formulate his letter and use a straight edge to draw his pencil lines across the card for writing.

"How many lines do you think that I will need, Leigh Anne?" asked Ralph.

"Well, that depends on much you would like to write, Ralph," I replied.

As his empathic heart began to recite what he wanted to write, I carefully penned every word on notebook paper. In turn, he copied every word in his very best penmanship and even included a drawing of a tiger paw, too!

"OK, Ralph, it looks like you are almost finished," I said. "I will address this for you and get it in the mail right away."

"Wait, Leigh Anne!" exclaimed Ralph. "I need to show you something."

Ralph has a knack for finding things to show me to extend his weekly lesson time.

"Ralph, we have already done quite a bit for today, and we are already over on our lesson time," I explained.

"I know, Leigh Anne, but I really need to show you something."

Reluctantly, I gave in to his pleading and said, "Well, OK, Ralph, but we really need to hurry so we can finish."

As he dug into his black, grocery recycling bag from our church, which he uses as his book bag, Ralph pulled out his new adult lesson book. He and our executive director, Nada Weekley, work together in this book, so I had not seen his assignment and thought he wanted to share.

Ralph quickly opened the workbook, and much to my surprise, his first lesson, complete with new vocabulary words across the top of the page, was all about the human heart.

As tears filled my eyes, I said, "Ralph, this is great. It's all about the heart."

"I told you that I needed to show you something, Leigh Anne," said Ralph.

"Do you want me to include this in your card?" I asked.

Ralph nodded, and I asked if he wanted to add an explanation.

"No, that's not necessary," said Ralph. "He [Barker] will know."

So, we finished up a sincere get well note to President Barker, which was complete with a tiger paw and a worksheet on the heart, and again, I silently prayed, "Thank you, God."

Hoover family at Clemson tailgate
Left to Right: Bradley, Leigh Anne, Jennifer and Brad

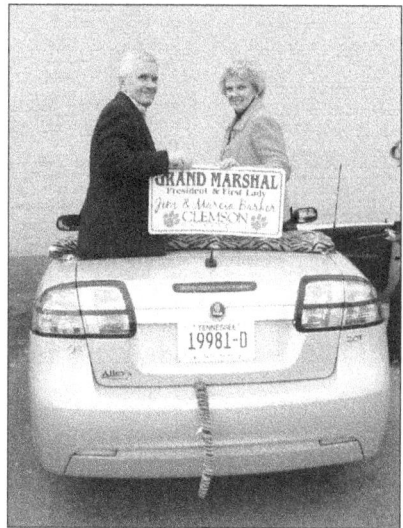

Clemson University President Jim Barker and wife Marcia following service as grand marshals for the Kingsport, Tennessee, Christmas parade

CHAPTER TWENTY-THREE

Clemson Coach Dabo Swinney

Clemson University also just happens to be blessed with a wonderful head football coach, Dabo Swinney, who admittedly experienced his share of personal trials and tribulations growing up in a dysfunctional family situation. However, throughout everything, Swinney trusted God's plan for his life. He attests that all of the early hardships and difficulties, which are now resolved, served to make him the person he is today. Swinney often shares his own, personal testimony of Christian faith.

As only God would have it, Swinney has been able to utilize his life experiences to touch many other lives. He attests to trusting in the Lord, God's grace and His ultimate plan to guide and direct his life. Swinney uses his professional position, which gives him the platform to truly make a difference, to glorify God.

In fact, Swinney shares if individuals will always put God first in everything, believe in themselves and never quit, they will find true success, peace and happiness, which come from God being within us through the Holy Spirit.

***

One day, when we were traveling to the Caribbean Island of St. Kitts, Brad and I had the pleasure of running into Coach Swinney and his wife, Kathleen. Immediately, Brad, and my youngest brother, Chris, also a Clemson alum, scrambled to get the Clemson "Tiger Rag" out of a suitcase to pose for a photo with Coach Swinney.

Brad told him we were from Kingsport, Tennessee, and they instantly began talking about Coty Sensabaugh and our shared Clemson connection. We would later learn that Swinney and Kathleen were also traveling on the same plane, along with several other coaches, for a Nike event on the neighboring island of Nevis. When we boarded the plane, they were the first people who greeted us. Both had big smiles, commented on my Clemson wardrobe colors and Swinney was reading the book *Lead . . . for God's Sake!* Was this a coincidence? I do not believe it was.

Swinney's mantra truly exemplifies Ralph's life. Like Ralph, he exudes the very same dedication and determination. Swinney knows God is directing his life.

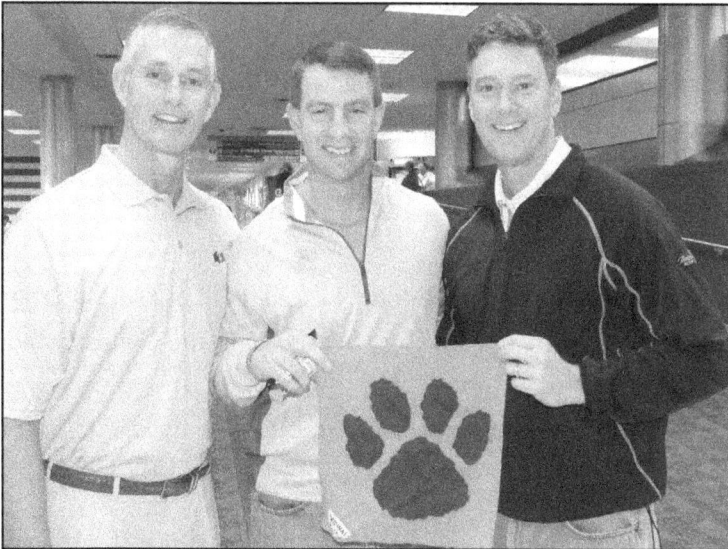

Brad Hoover, Clemson Head Football Coach Dabo Swinney and Chris Whitlock in the airport

CHAPTER TWENTY-FOUR

Reptiles

R alph's love for Clemson even extended over to his passion for reptiles. For a short while, he owned a corn snake he purchased and named "Clemson" for its orange coloring. Each week, I endured stories about the snake. However, when it came to discussing the snake's diet, I quickly drew the line.

"Leigh Anne, Clemson is doing great," said Ralph. "You should see him!"

"Now, who is Clemson, Ralph?" I asked. "I'm not sure what you're talking about. Do you mean Coty Sensabaugh, the Clemson football player?"

"No, Clemson is my new snake, and he is orange," said Ralph.

"Why did you get a snake, Ralph?" I asked. "I thought that you liked your toads."

"I do, Leigh Anne," answered Ralph. "But, you see, I'm really part reptile, and I'm cold-blooded."

"No, you're not, Ralph," I said. "You're warm blooded and a mammal like all humans, and I think that you've been watching too many episodes of 'Animal Planet.' What does your snake eat?"

"Mice," said Ralph. "But, don't worry, Leigh Anne. He doesn't eat very often."

Ralph studying about another favorite reptile, the sea turtle, in *Turtle Summer* by Mary Alice Monroe

CHAPTER TWENTY-FIVE

Mice

In addition to my many germ phobias, I also do not care for snakes and mice, but for a little while, I humored Ralph by engaging him in conversation about his new pet snake, Clemson.

Weekly lessons always begin with conversation about Ralph's week and what's going on in his life. So, I decided that if I did not have to see the actual pet snake, I could, at least, talk about him with Ralph.

"So, Ralph, how's your snake doing?" I asked.

"Great, great, Leigh Anne," said Ralph. "Clemson is good, and now I have two mice."

"Did you say 'two' mice?" I asked.

"Yep, I have a male and a female," replied Ralph. "I am going to be a breeder."

Apparently, the corn snake was eating mice that were purchased from the pet store and kept frozen until needed for the snake. This was more information than I ever needed to know, but Ralph had decided he could become a breeder and eliminate this step.

"Where did you get these two mice, Ralph?" I asked.

"Well, I caught one behind the bank in a field, and I got the other one near a drain spout," said Ralph. "If I am a breeder, this will save me money."

Ralph is also a member of our Sunday school class, and often, he will bring in objects for show and tell. His way of interacting with the class is to pass things around our room to share. Usually, this consists of his postcards. However, the next week, he had something in a plastic grocery bag.

"What do you have to share today, Ralph?" I asked.

"Oh, look, Leigh Anne. It's a mouse trap," replied Ralph.

As I glanced at the bag, Ralph immediately saw the expression on my face.

"What's wrong, Leigh Anne?" he asked.

When I looked at the Havaheart trap with photos of mice on the sides, I quickly discouraged his passing around this item.

"Ralph, I will talk to you about this later, but I do not think you should pass around the mouse trap," I said.

"OK. I understand, Leigh Anne, and you're probably right," said Ralph. "But, don't worry 'cause it doesn't kill the mouse."

The next week, Ralph and I talked extensively about his own germ phobias and the idea that having a snake for a pet and catching mice was probably not the best idea. He actually agreed, and, thankfully, the pet store took Clemson, the corn snake, back for another interested customer.

CHAPTER TWENTY-SIX

Another Library Card

With Ralph's continual fascination with reptiles, I decided he might enjoy visiting the library to actually check out a book.

"Ralph, do you have a library card?" I asked.

"Yep, I sure do," said Ralph as he pulled out his wallet.

The card looked like it was old, but he proudly displayed it for me.

"Hey, you sure do!" I said. "I bet that you might need a new one. I'm going to the library after our lesson. Do you want to come with me?"

"Sure, Leigh Anne," said Ralph. "I guess I can go to the library."

Following our lesson, the two of us drove over to the library. When we approached the front desk, a lady assisted me with checking out the novel I had on hold and then asked how she might help Ralph.

"Well, he has a library card, but I bet that he needs a new one," I explained.

Ralph proudly pulled his card out of his worn wallet, and the lady began checking the number in the computer. Apparently, he was no longer listed in the system, which normally would not be a problem, but Ralph needed additional identification.

"Don't worry. I've got a photo ID, Leigh Anne!" exclaimed Ralph excitedly as he pulled out his Tennessee identification card.

"This will work, but we will also need something else," said the library employee.

Disappointed, Ralph searched his billfold for another form of identification. Yet, there was nothing that would suffice.

Sensing his frustration, I immediately explained he was my adult reading student and asked if there might be a way to avoid this step and get him another library card. Obviously, he had been authorized to have one in the past. However, since the system showed no record of his name and number, it was as if he had never been approved.

Upon hearing our discussion, another library employee came over and mentioned that a piece of cancelled mail would also work. Immediately, a light came on and a window was opened.

"Ralph, do you know what this means?" I asked with excitement.

"No, what, Leigh Anne?" he replied.

"We can use one of your postcards!" I exclaimed. "That's a piece of cancelled mail!"

With the widest smile I had ever seen, Ralph immediately said he would go to my car and get one out of his book bag. Afraid the car alarm might go off accidentally and frighten him and make bystanders think that Ralph was possibly breaking into my car, I suggested we go together.

On our way out to the car, Ralph was so excited.

"Can you believe it, Ralph?" I asked. "You have mail that has your name and address on it, and this will help you get a library card."

"I know, Leigh Anne," Ralph replied. "I don't know what you want me to say."

"You don't have to say anything, Ralph. This is great!"

Silently, I said another prayer of thanks to God.

CHAPTER TWENTY-SEVEN

Sea Turtles and Author Mary Alice Monroe

B eing a "reptile man," Ralph is also interested in turtles, and this fascination links us to another God connection.

The summer that my mother was in what was to become her final stages of cancer, I could have never imagined that the accidental reading of a novel would also connect and enhance the path of my life forever, but isn't that exactly how the Holy Spirit always works?

Earlier that summer, I had expressed an interest in reading *The Beach House* by James Patterson and Peter de Jonge. So, when Bradley, our son, was over at our next-door neighbor's house, and he saw the book that he thought I wanted to read, our neighbor told him to take it home and let me read it. She also said to just bring it back when I finished.

Since he remembered the title, Bradley was excited to bring in a paperback copy of *The Beach House,* and I never let on that this was a different book. Rather, I thanked him and bragged on him for thinking of me and remembering. I also set aside the novel, which was by Mary Alice Monroe, thinking I would read it one day.

Little did I realize, *The Beach House* by Mary Alice Monroe was, in fact, the novel that I was truly meant to read, and it would touch my life and enrich it in ways I could have never, ever begun to imagine.

As fate would have it, I began reading the novel. In fact, I was well into it when we went to the beach as a family, and I hid it from my mother, who was a voracious reader, because the mother in the novel was dying from cancer.

Since my own mother also had cancer, I wanted to shelter her from this precious book. Yet, curiosity got to her, too, and I actually caught her sneaking and reading one afternoon. To this day, for all I know, she probably read the entire novel and even understood my concern.

Once you begin a Monroe novel, it's hard to resist the lure that she depicts through her lyrical language as she eloquently weaves together events in nature that parallel human relationships. From loggerhead sea turtles, to birds of prey, sweetgrass, monarch butterflies, the shrimping industry, dolphins and many others, Monroe captivates and endears readers as she also educates through her body of work.

In *The Beach House*, the parallel is with a mother-daughter relationship and the loggerhead sea turtle, who comes ashore to lay her eggs yet never returns to the nest.

Although my mother and I shared a very close relationship throughout her life, as an adult, I now realize that some women search their entire lives to find what we had. Even though she passed away at just 67, and I sincerely wish that she were still alive, I feel blessed for that special bond.

After reading *The Beach House*, I devoured every Monroe novel I could find, and I was elated to learn that she would be speaking at an event in South Carolina. The day that I heard her speak, I could barley suppress my tears.

My daughter, Jennifer, commented that her approach to writing sounded exactly like mine. As a former journalist and teacher, it is important for Monroe to include factual information in her novels, and she also educates and writes children's books in the very same manner.

At that time, her first children's book, *Turtle Summer*, which is the companion to the adult novel, *The Beach House*, had been recently released, and I was able to purchase a copy that would become part of my teaching materials.

Following her program, I purchased a new, signed copy of *The Beach House* for my neighbor, and Monroe even signed the one that I had cherished for years. The two of us chatted, and it was as if we had always known each other. We felt a kindred bond, and the two of us became friends.

I would go on to write about her passion for the Sea Turtle Hospital in Charleston, and she endorsed my children's books, *The Santa Train Tradition* and *Festus and His Fun Fest Favorites*. With a shared connection to literacy and education, I included her endorsement and her work when I spoke at the Tennessee Association of School Librarians Conference.

During one of my breakout sessions, when I mentioned Monroe's endorsement and her first foray into children's books, I noticed a lady feverishly searching through her tote bag and pulling out a copy of *Swimming Lessons*, which is Monroe's sequel to *The Beach House* and takes place at the Sea Turtle Hospital in Charleston, South Carolina.

Astounded, I simply smiled after noticing the novel and included another silent pray of thanks. Was this merely a coincidence? I truly do not believe that it was.

Later that year, Monroe and I planned an opportunity to have her come to Kingsport for a fundraiser for the Literacy Council. We held hands in her living room and vowed to make it happen.

In order to host an event, at that time, you really needed to have at least 100 in attendance. So, I carried her bookmarks with me everywhere and talked to anyone who would listen. I knew if people read my friend's books, they, too, would love her work. Plus, our organization needed 100 interested supporters.

Originally, I had hoped to have her visit in conjunction with the release of *The Butterfly's Daughter*. Monroe's tour representatives had booked her for an event in South Carolina, and she would only be about two and a half hours away from Kingsport. However, the details for an event in Kingsport just never seemed to materialize.

I was really frustrated because she was going to be so close, and in my mind, this should have worked. So, we decided to put plans on the "back burner" and postpone the event.

Little did I realize that the neighboring state's event would ultimately be cancelled, and we would have been saddled with an event that was not part of a book tour, which typically means a much pricier event. For a non-profit organization, this would have negated our fundraising efforts and been devastating.

So much for my plan! God definitely had another one.

Ultimately, the Monroe appearance we would host was well off the beaten path and to be included as part of her book tour for none other than *New York Times* bestselling novel, *Beach House Memories*, which is the prequel to her *New York Times* bestseller, *The Beach House*. However, Kingsport made the tour, and over 200 people were in attendance!

Kingsport's Mayor Dennis Phillips proclaimed May 18, 2012, as "Literacy Legacy Day" in Kingsport, and he presented Monroe with a key to the city. It was a glorious day and an answered prayer. Ralph was on hand as a volunteer worker, and he finally had the opportunity to meet the "Turtle Lady!"

Kingsport Mayor Dennis Phillips presents *New York Times* bestselling author Mary Alice Monroe with a key to the city.

CHAPTER TWENTY-EIGHT

Ralph and the "Turtle Lady"

After covering the Sea Turtle Hospital in Charleston, South Carolina, and interviewing Monroe about her involvement and connection through her *Swimming Lessons* novel, I had collected lots of interesting pictures to share with Ralph. I could not wait to show him the photos of the turtles being rehabilitated in their individual swimming pools and tell him about the different types of turtle patients I saw.

I even had my picture taken beside an outside sculpture of a frog. Or, was it a toad? Either way, it was a whimsical version, so I knew that Ralph would just shake his head and declare that I was crazy.

It was also the perfect time to share Monroe's children's book, *Turtle Summer*, and I knew that with Ralph's love of reptiles, the loggerhead sea turtle information would be very interesting to him.

The timing was also leading up to Monroe's book tour stop in Kingsport, so Ralph was hearing lots about her in the Literacy Council office. Volunteers were reading her novels, and now, he was reading one of her books, too.

"Ralph, I cannot wait for you to see my pictures from the Sea Turtle Hospital," I said. As I shuffled through my book bag collecting my photos and my book, Ralph quickly grabbed a postcard.

"Are you talking about this, Leigh Anne?" asked Ralph holding up a postcard from the South Carolina Aquarium.

"Oh, great, Ralph!" I exclaimed. "I see that you received the postcard that we sent from our visit. Yes, that's where we were and where the Sea Turtle Hospital is located, and you will have to read that to me, but I also have other photos to show you."

As I fanned the photos out of the turtles, I could sense his excitement. "You saw these?" asked Ralph. "What's wrong with them?"

"Well, that's a good question, Ralph," I said. "Many were hurt in various accidents at sea. Some were caught in shrimp nets, others were hit by boat propellers, and some were just sick and washed ashore with the tide. At the Sea Turtle Hospital, they are kept in individual tanks that look like swimming pools until they can be rehabilitated and released back into the ocean."

"Really, Leigh Anne?" asked Ralph. "I didn't know that."

He carefully studied each photo and was interested in reading the types of turtle patients listed on the photo of the patient board.

"Do you remember hearing about my friend Mary Alice Monroe?" I asked.

"Yes," said Ralph. "Why?"

"Well, in addition to being a writer, she also volunteers and helps with the sea turtles."

"She does?" asked Ralph. "That means she's a 'turtle lady'! Oh, I'm sorry, Leigh Anne. I didn't mean to say that."

"No, that's OK, Ralph," I explained. "Actually, Mary Alice is a turtle lady. That's what they call the ladies who walk the beach and monitor the nests. In fact, I have a new book to share with you today that she wrote and will teach you all about it. Do you want to read it?"

As I pulled out the signed hardback version of *Turtle Summer*, Ralph gingerly took the book in his hands and started turning the colorful pages.

"Leigh Anne, will you help me?" asked Ralph.

"Sure," I said "We can take turns."

Another silent prayer of "thank you, God," was prayed.

Being the minimalist that he is, Ralph suggested that I keep the book. We continued to include *Turtle Summer* as a part of his weekly lesson, and he had his very own photo bookmark of Mary Alice. In fact, he even requested a second one, which was very special. He wanted to put one on his refrigerator, but he also needed a magnet!

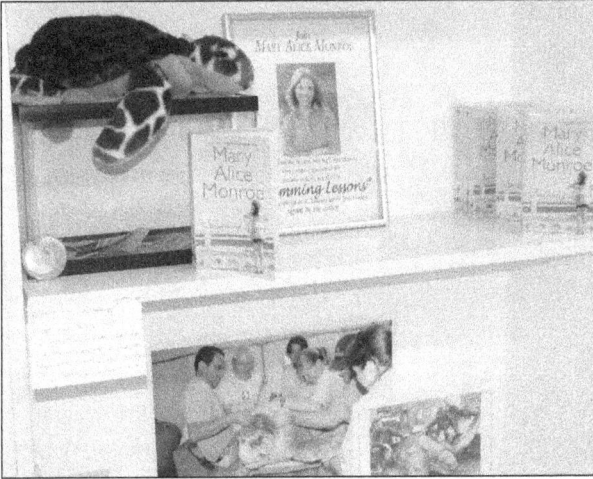

Sea Turtle Hospital at the South Carolina Aquarium— setting for Monroe's novel *Swimming Lessons*

Leigh Anne W. Hoover poses for a "frog" photo for Ralph after covering the Sea Turtle Hospital.

CHAPTER TWENTY-NINE

Ralph meets Mary Alice Monroe

Of course, I kept Mary Alice in the loop on my adult reading student and his desire to meet her, and she looked forward to it. When the day of the event finally arrived, Ralph planned to work as a volunteer.

I knew that I would be tied up with lots of event details, so I enlisted Brad and Bradley, who was in from Clemson, to help, and I also included Ralph.

Bradley picked up Ralph, and he stepped out in his white jeans, blue dress shirt and a tie. Ralph was dressed up for the event.

"Hey, Bradley, my friend!" exclaimed Ralph. "Are you going to meet the turtle lady? I mean Mary Alice Monroe?"

"Sure thing, Ralph," said Bradley. "Glad you are coming, too."

"I don't really like hotels, Bradley," said Ralph. "And, it's hot in your truck."

"Just roll down your window," replied Bradley.

As soon as they arrived at the MeadowView Marriot Resort Conference and Convention Center, Ralph quickly forgot all about his complaints, and he made his way to the meet and greet.

Mary Alice was visiting with sponsors and hostesses for the event when Ralph came in the room. Even though he attends church, Ralph usually avoids crowds and stays to himself. I knew that this was out of his comfort zone, but he also really wanted to meet her.

When Ralph spotted me, I immediately grabbed the *Turtle Summer* book from my things and went over to meet him.

"Well, hello, Ralph," I said. "You look very nice."

"Thanks. Thank you, Leigh Anne," said Ralph. "I came to meet Mary Alice."

"I know, Ralph, and I thought you might want to pose for a photo with her book that we read."

"OK, Leigh Anne, if that's what you want me to do," said Ralph.

Nervously, Ralph took the hardback book from me, and we made our way over the book signing table. He also had one of her bookmarks stuck in his shirt pocket.

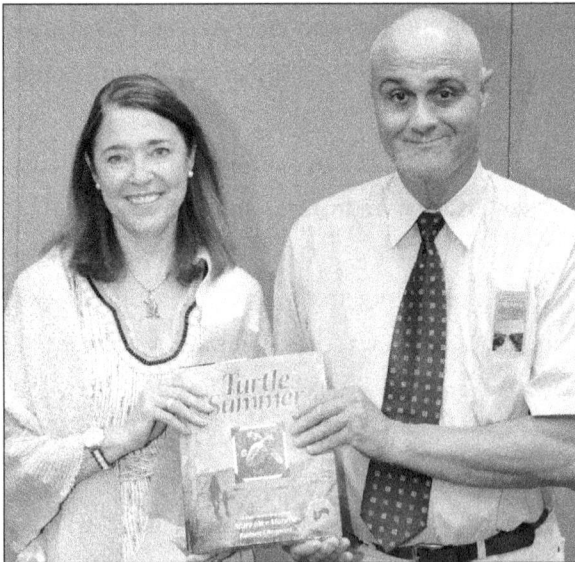

New York Times bestselling author Mary Alice Monroe and Ralph
(Photo by: Brian Hullette/VIPSEEN Magazine)

Of course, Mary Alice was so very welcoming and very excited to meet Ralph. The whole time that she greeted him and praised Ralph for his reading efforts, he smiled the biggest smile I have ever seen. Not only was he meeting a *New York Times* bestselling author, Ralph was also meeting his hero, the "turtle lady," and he was proud of her. They had made a connection through literacy, and I prayed a silent thank you to God.

Following her visit, Mary Alice printed a special note to Ralph on an event poster and even printed her name so that he could read it. Today, both the poster and their photo together are framed and hanging in his small apartment. Their photo together also made the regional *VIPSeen Magazine* in an article about the event.

***

"Ralph, guess what?" I asked as I spotted Ralph downtown several weeks later.

"Leigh Anne, you scared me," said Ralph. "What's wrong?"

"Nothing, Ralph," I replied. "Your picture with Mary Alice is in a magazine."

"I know, Leigh Anne. They have already shown me at Wallace News," said Ralph.

"Well, that's great! Have you ever been in a magazine?"

"Yea, Leigh Anne, about two times," said Ralph.

Knowing that Ralph was thinking about his photo in another publication, I quickly replied, "Not the church directory, Ralph. I'm talking about a real magazine."

Since that meeting, the two have also exchanged letters. Ralph wanted to express his thanks to Mary Alice, so he wrote a note, and I personally delivered it to her. She also sent a reply to Ralph in the mail and included a special bookmark just for him.

The day that I gave Mary Alice the note, we were on Daufuskie Island, South Carolina, a favorite beach getaway my Hoover family calls home. I also met her friend, fellow *New York Times* bestselling author, Patti Callahan Henry.

Mary Alice wanted me to meet her, and knowing that Patti would also be there; I plowed through her work in preparation and learned more about her connection to Daufuskie, an island she references as "Oystertip" Island in her novels. As the daughter of a minister, Patti also often references the Holy Spirit in her writing.

Like Mary Alice, Patti was also touched by Ralph's sentiments. As she read the letter, Patti mentioned to Mary Alice that Ralph noted being proud of Mary Alice and appreciative of her work with the sea turtles.

It was a great day, planned by God, and I said another silent prayer of thanks.

Today, Ralph is looking forward to learning all about the monarch butterfly in Mary Alice's new children's book, *A Butterfly Called Hope*, and he has specially requested one be written about her dolphin research, too!

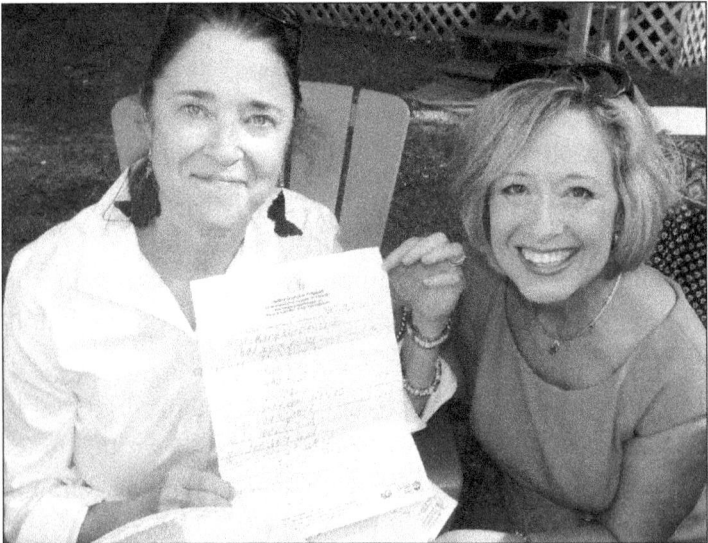

New York Times bestselling author Mary Alice Monroe and local author Leigh Anne W. Hoover with Ralph's letter on Daufuskie Island, SC

CHAPTER THIRTY

Reading Aloud

R alph was raised as a worshipping Catholic, and one of his possessions is a *New Saint Joseph Children's Missal with Hymns.* According to the book's inscription, it serves as "an easy way of participating in Mass for boys and girls," and the copyright date is 1968. Despite learning disabilities, Ralph can remember his father reading to him.

The Literacy Council of Kingsport, Incorporated is a program of the United Way of Greater Kingsport, which has recently identified early grade reading as the number one cause of community service and human health needs and is serving to remedy this situation in our region.

With my two children's books, *The Santa Train Tradition* and *Festus and His Fun Fest Favorites*, I have appreciated the opportunity to expose children to reading by connecting them to actual events in our community.

My philosophy on reading, especially reading aloud, totally changed in 1994 when I met Jim Trelease, author of *New York Times* bestseller

The Read-Aloud Handbook. I always knew reading to children was important, but Trelease truly opened my eyes and connected me to just how important.

With our two children, we read many stories. Bradley always enjoyed *Peter Pan*, and we read this one many times. His sister endured the experience because Jennifer did not like hearing about the pirates—especially nightly. Well, I decided to remedy that situation and just eliminate that part of the story.

Of course, my plan ended abruptly when a little hand touched the book, and in an emphatic voice, Bradley said, "Don't skip the pirates! Mama, you skipped the pirates."

Trelease helped me focus on which stories were good to read aloud and to read individually. Even when children are not able to read chapter books themselves, they are able to listen. Listening increases vocabularies and ultimately strengthens reading comprehension by hearing new words in context. Trelease also encourages continuing reading aloud even when children are older.

Bradley certainly benefited from Trelease's visit to Kingsport, and the two of us went on to read classics aloud like *Where the Red Fern Grows* and *Summer of the Monkeys* by Wilson Rawls. For my outdoorsman, Gary Paulson was another one of his favorite authors.

With this in mind, I have tried to always incorporate reading aloud in my lessons with Ralph. Although Ralph reads to me, I also read aloud to him.

After he reads from the selected Laubach Bible materials, I always find the same verses in an adolescent Bible and reread the passages to Ralph. He loves to finish and just listen.

With this in mind, and following Trelease's advice on finding materials that highlight a child or student's interests, I found something of interest to Ralph.

Ralph and author Leigh Anne W. Hoover with her children's books, which also benefit the Literacy Council of Kingsport

Ralph at the Literacy Council of Kingsport

CHAPTER THIRTY-ONE

Reptiles Magazine

As an adult reading student, Ralph may be our only one with three tutors. Although each of us helps him on a different level, Ralph has enlisted the help of three, and each of us has stayed with him throughout his reading journey.

Since Ralph's reading has improved from a first grade level to that of a solid sixth grade student, I thought he might enjoy receiving a magazine. Even though we are truly in a digital age, magazines of all types have managed to hang on for tactile learners and readers, and there's even one that features reptiles.

Knowing this would appeal to him, and we could incorporate it in our weekly lessons, I decided to investigate a possible subscription. That fall, one of my nieces was selling magazine subscriptions as a fundraiser for her school, and it just so happened that *REPTILES* magazine was on the list. I decided to order a subscription for Ralph as one of his Christmas presents, and I told him that he would be receiving that part of his present monthly in the mail.

Of course, from then on, Ralph would ask me about it each week.

"Leigh Anne, when is my magazine coming?" asked Ralph.

"Oh, I am sure that you will be getting it soon, Ralph," I replied. "I bet that it will come in the mail after the first of the year."

We engaged in this same conversation for several weeks until the first issue finally arrived. As expected, Ralph took his magazine around town to show anyone and everyone who wanted to see it. Because he could read some of the sentences and words from the articles, he also thought that he was quite the authority on reptiles, and he would eagerly tell you this, too.

In addition to interesting articles, *REPTILES* magazine also contains colorful photographs of a variety of unusual reptiles, and this prompted Ralph to add to his pet family.

Like a child, he was intrigued by the geckos and quickly added "Opossum" and "Shorty," which were the names of his new geckos, to his growing reptile collection.

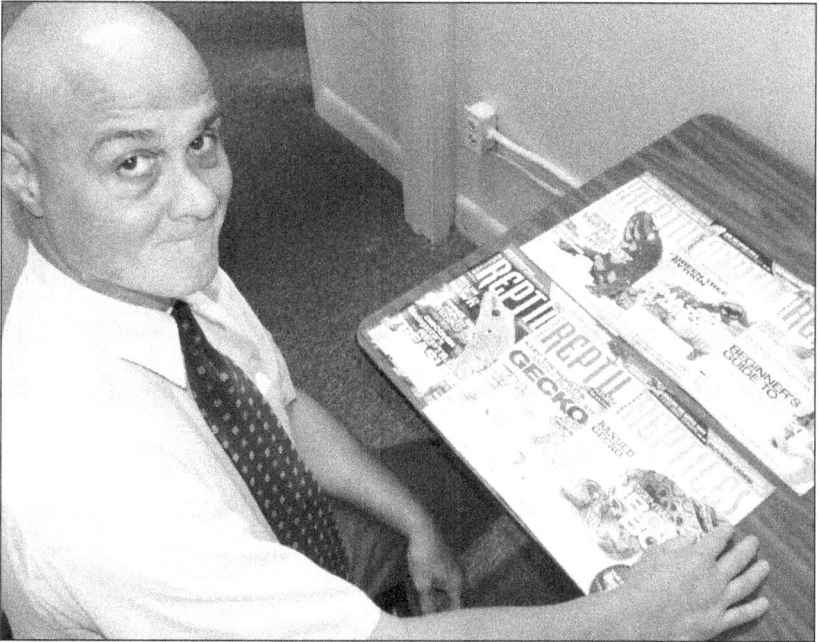

Ralph proudly displays his *REPTILES* magazine collection.

CHAPTER THIRTY-TWO

Teaching Other Sunday School Classes

As a member of our Inquirers Sunday school class at First Broad Street United Methodist Church in Kingsport, Tennessee, Ralph takes part in many activities with the class, and one of these activities includes teaching. Couples take turns with lessons, and when Brad and I teach, Ralph joins us at the front of the class.

It took several lessons before he felt comfortable contributing. However, now he will gladly read his copy of "The Lord's Prayer" to close our lesson with the class.

Even though Ralph reads this to me each week following our tutoring session, he had rarely read it in another setting. The first time that I told him we would be teaching and asked Ralph to bring his copy of the prayer, he forgot it. So, the next time we taught, I made a copy of his large print version and made sure I included it in my teaching materials. To make sure Ralph would come to Sunday school, I waited to tell him it was our turn to teach and shared the prayer with him on that Sunday.

This worked, and Ralph read "The Lord's Prayer" aloud to our class.

Thank you, God.

Ralph and I have also shared our testimony with other Sunday school classes. This has helped to not only show how God has been at work in our life journeys, but it has also connected Ralph to others in our church family.

When I asked Ralph if he would like to do this, I explained that he would have an opportunity to talk if he wanted to share.

"OK, Leigh Anne," said Ralph. "You will let me know when to go... right?"

"Of course, Ralph. Don't you worry," I replied.

Brad accompanied us that morning, and he sat with Ralph while I spoke and shared our story. As we neared time to conclude, I told the class I had asked Ralph to also share a few words.

When Ralph approached the front of the class, my heart was filled with pride and love for this man's accomplishments and his willingness to share. He had come such a long way, yet I could never have anticipated what would happen next.

As he began to go back in time with his life story, I realized that I may not have explained myself correctly. We were nearing the end of class time, and Ralph was on a roll.

"Ralph," I interrupted. "You may want to just give a few highlights because we are going to have to end soon so that everyone can go to worship."

"Leigh Anne," said Ralph. "What do you mean? I just got started, and you have been talking the entire time!"

Of course, the class erupted in laughter as Ralph shook his head at me in frustration.

"Well, I am sure that if you would like to say more, we might just have to come back another week," I explained.

Thank you, God.

CHAPTER THIRTY-THREE

Left at the Altar

On occasion, our minister will have an altar call. Even though the altar is always open for prayer, sometimes there is a special call of invitation.

The first time this happened, I could tell Ralph had heard, and he wanted to go. An associate minister was leaving, and he had been close to her. So, I asked if he wanted to go down, and I told Ralph I would go with him.

When we began working with Ralph at the Literacy Council, we realized he was having difficulties hearing, and this impaired his progress. In fact, he originally wanted to learn to read so he could read the closed captioning on his television.

He also was experiencing some visual difficulties and needed glasses.

We were able to help him get a hearing aid, and the Lions Club actually paid for his glasses. When he wears both, he does really well, but Ralph is also quite vain. He always carries his glasses, reading glasses and hearing aids in his book bag, but he does not always wear them—especially on Sundays.

One Sunday, we had an altar call during worship and, again, I sensed Ralph wanted to go down front. Brad was serving as an usher that week, so the two of us were seated together. I mouthed that I would go down front with him. Ralph managed to get out in the aisle to let me go first, but I never realized he sat back down.

As I knelt at the altar, I quickly sensed I was by myself. Our senior minister, Mickey Rainwater, knelt down and asked if he might pray with me.

"I believe that you had better," I replied. "Ralph was supposed to join me at the altar, but I see that he has left me with this. So, please pray for our ministry together."

Knowing Ralph and relieved, Reverend Rainwater smiled, and he said a beautiful prayer asking God to continue guiding and directing me in my work with Ralph.

Ralph poses beside his church home signage in Kingsport, Tennessee.

CHAPTER THIRTY-FOUR

Going Forward

I am sure Ralph and I will continue to grow in our journey together, and I hope that I can tutor him for many years to come.

As we have become closer, often, I will ask Ralph if he's my friend. He always gets emotional and explains we are much more than friends. We are brothers and sisters in Christ.

When Ralph learned I was writing a book about him, he simply said, "This book is not about me, Leigh Anne. It's about God."

And, I said, "Amen!"

Afterword

BY PASTOR MICKEY RAINWATER

I have the special blessing of being the pastor of the church Leigh Anne references throughout *Reading with Ralph.* I am a very blessed man to be the spiritual leader of such an amazing congregation where people find so many wonderful ways to live out their calling as followers of Jesus. I am blessed that I also get to be the pastor of both Leigh Anne and her family, and of Ralph. What amazing people they are!

I am struck, as I hope you have been as you've read this book, at how God uses us in ways we never anticipated; working with our gifts, our growing edges and our anxieties. In *Reading with Ralph* we were able to see how two people have continued the life long journey of growing into the greater fullness of who God created us to be.

While I see both Leigh Anne and Ralph moving about the church, I have learned so much about each of them. Thank you, Leigh Anne, for being willing to be transparent with your readers in order to tell the story of this remarkable relationship.

I had all but forgotten the Sunday which Leigh Anne relates of believing she was accompanying Ralph to the altar rail for a time of prayer, only to experience the awkwardness of being "left at the altar." (The memory brought a smile to my face.) I am also mindful of those times when Ralph has come to the church to read and to get a cup of coffee. I greet him, he responds, and I often call him

"Sir;" to which he lights up and says back to me, "I like it when you call me 'Sir'."

Reading with Ralph reminds us that our journey often connects us with people we never anticipated, in ways we never expected; and that is appropriate. After all, are we not all children of the same Father?

– Mickey Rainwater
First Broad Street United Methodist Church, Senior Pastor

LITERACY COUNCIL

When Ralph Buck came to the Literacy Council of Kingsport, he was at a first grade reading level. Today, through dedication and determination, he is above a sixth grade level and continues to improve.

As for many new literates, reading has opened a new world for Ralph. He has a new sense of freedom and independence, which has also given him increased confidence in social situations.

According to the U. S. Department of Education, National Institute of Literacy, 32 million U.S. adults cannot read. Illiterate adults are not able to complete job applications, read road signs, cooking directions or even instructions for taking medications.

As a nation, illiteracy leads to unemployment, poverty, homelessness, crime and so many other woes. However, you can help. By becoming an adult tutor, you can make a difference and help end illiteracy.

A portion of the proceeds from the sale of this book will benefit the Literacy Council of Kingsport, Inc.

For additional information on how you can become involved, please contact your local Literacy Council or visit ProLiteracy at www.proliteracy.org

MARY ALICE MONROE

Dear Ralph,
  Thank you for your great letter. I'm proud that you hung a poster of my book in your house!
  The turtle season is over and we can relax until they return in the spring.
  I hope you have a wonderful Christmas!

I wish you peace and joy.

                    Much love,
                    Mary Alice

Nov. 23, 2012

12/5/2011

Dear Ralph:

Someone told me you are a Clemson fan. I saw your picture reading about Coty Sensabaugh in the Kingsport paper. Kingsport is my hometown, too. So we have two things in common.

Best wishes from Clemson and Go Tigers!

PRESIDENT'S HOME

President's Home
Clemson University

Sketch by Jim Barker

The president's residence at Clemson University, located near the east entrance to campus, was completed in 1958. Designed in the classic revival style, the home is built of white-painted brick and features tall white columns at the front.
In 1979 the interior was totally renovated, and the garage was converted into a family room.
Flowering dogwood, crape myrtle, maple, hemlock and stately magnolia trees, interspersed with roses, azaleas, rhododendron and other flowering plants, surround the home. Five Clemson presidents have lived in the home and hosted official functions of the University.

About the Author

Leigh Anne W. Hoover is a native of Spartanburg, South Carolina, and a graduate of Clemson University. With a bachelor of arts degree in secondary education/English and a minor in general communications, Hoover has worked for over 30 years in the media. She has extensive writing, speaking and public relations experience in the region and has

Author Leigh Anne W. Hoover teaching with Festus reading buddy

published articles encompassing personality and home profiles, arts and entertainment reviews, medical topics and weekend escape pieces.

Notable features include one-on-one interviews with actress Andie MacDowell, artists Bob Timberlake and P. Buckley Moss, author Jan Karon, Grammy-winner, singer/songwriter Kenny Loggins and Clemson University President James F. Barker. Hoover also writes a monthly column for East Tennessee Medical News titled "Enjoying East Tennessee."

She is the author of the well-known children's book *The Santa Train Tradition* and award-winning *Festus and His Fun Fest Favorites*. Her children's books have been endorsed by *New York Times* bestselling author Mary Alice Monroe and parent educator Nancy Samalin. *Reading with Ralph – A Journey in Christian Compassion* is her third book.

Hoover serves on the Literacy Council of Kingsport and Friends of Allandale board of directors and is a member of the Kingsport Delphian Club. She is also a past president of the Literacy Council of Kingsport, the Junior League of Kingsport and past co-chair of the Clemson University Parents' Development Board.

Hoover is a member of First Broad Street United Methodist Church, and she volunteers as an adult reading tutor. She and her husband, Brad, reside in Kingsport, and they have two adult children.

Contact her via email at hoover@chartertn.net, Facebook at www.facebook.com/LeighAnneWHoover or www.thesantatraintradition.com.

Leigh Anne W. Hoover is also the author of two children's books

The Santa Train Tradition

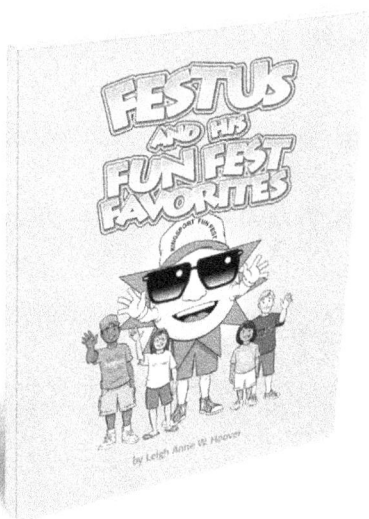

Written by
Leigh Anne W. Hoover

Illustrated by
Carol Baker Murray

Festus and His Fun Fest Favorites

by Leigh Anne W. Hoover

International Festivals &
Event Association –
2010 Pinnacle Award
Northeast Tennessee
Tourism Association –
2011 Pinnacle Award

**Available at www.wordofmouthpress.us
and/or www.thesantatraintradition.com**

www.ingramcontent.com/pod-product-compliance
Lightning Source LLC
Chambersburg PA
CBHW031518040426
42445CB00009B/295